THE SONG OF SONGS

BERIT OLAM
Studies in Hebrew Narrative & Poetry

The Song
of Songs

Dianne Bergant, C.S.A.

David W. Cotter, O.S.B.
Editor

Jerome T. Walsh
Chris Franke
Associate Editors

A Michael Glazier Book

THE LITURGICAL PRESS
Collegeville, Minnesota

www.litpress.org

A Michael Glazier Book published by The Liturgical Press.

Cover design by Ann Blattner.

1   2   3   4   5   6   7   8   9

Library of Congress Cataloging-in-Publication Data

Bergant, Dianne.
  The Song of songs / Dianne Bergant ; David W. Cotter, editor.
      p.   cm.—(Berit Olam)
  Includes bibliographical references and index.
  ISBN 0-8146-5069-4 (alk. paper)
    1. Bible. O.T. Song of Solomon—Commentaries.   I. Cotter, David W.
  II. Title.   III. Series.

  BS1485.53 .B47   2001
  223'.9077—dc21

                                                            2001016507

CONTENTS

INTRODUCTION

Canonicity, Authorship, and Interpretation

The very name of this biblical book, the Song of Songs *(šîr haššîrîm)*, both reveals and obscures its identity. It is a *šîr* or lyric song, but not a *mizmōr* or religious poem, as are most of the biblical psalms that are also classified as *šîr* (Psalm 46 is an exception to this dual identification). Religious poems are frequently lyric in form, and so the Song of Songs can rightfully be considered either a religious work or a secular composition. The relative clause "which is Solomon's" *(ʾăšer lîšlōmōh)*[1] adds to the ambiguity of the Song of Songs. While the preposition *lĕ* is usually considered *lamed auctoris*, attributing authorship (see Psalms 72; 122), in Ugaritic poetry it simply means "concerning." Thus, the very construction implies that the Song of Songs can be regarded as either actually coming from the Judean king, or dealing with issues that were somehow associated with him. These alternative translations have yielded a variety of interpretations.

The book is renowned both for the unrestrained passion that it portrays and for the extravagant sensuousness of its imagery. While its eroticism may be expressed figuratively in Hebrew, it is often more explicit in the Greek translation. From earliest times the appropriateness of the Song of Songs as religious literature has been a point of controversy.[2] Rabbi Akiba (ca. 50–135 C.E.) championed the place of the Song of Songs in the canon by arguing:

---

[1] English translations are based on the New Revised Standard Version (NRSV) unless otherwise noted.

[2] For a discussion of the canonicity of the Song of Songs see Pardes, *Countertraditions in the Bible*, 118–43.

> Heaven forbid! No one in Israel ever disputed that the Song of Songs de-
> files the hands [that is, is sacred]. All the world is not worth the day that
> the Song of Songs was given to Israel; all the writings *(Kĕtûbîm)* are holy
> but the Song of Songs is the holy of holies (Mishnah *Yadaim* 3:5).

It was at this same time that Akiba also scathingly condemned the practice of using the Song of Songs in the taverns as a drinking ditty:

> Whoever trills his voice singing the Song of Songs in a banquet hall, re-
> garding it as a common song *(zĕmîr)*, has no part in the world to come
> (Tosefta *Sanhedrin* 12:10; see Babylonian Talmud *Sanhedrin* 101a).

A later passage attributed to Rabbi Simeon ben Gamaliel (ca. 140 C.E.)
describes Jerusalemite girls clad in white dresses dancing in the vineyards at harvest time, crying out to the men:

> Fellow, look around and see—choose what you want! Don't look for
> beauty, look for family. And so the Song of Songs (3:11) says, "Go forth
> you daughters of Zion, and behold King Solomon with the crown with
> which his mother crowned him in the day of his espousals and in the day
> of the gladness of his heart" (Mishnah *Taanith* 4:8).

This reference from rabbinic writings suggests that portions of the Song
of Songs were incorporated into harvest festivals, when young women
and men celebrated together in a relatively carefree manner. However,
these festivals were cultic celebrations, thus situating the flirtatious
activity squarely in the center of religious practice. This link with the
cult is corroborated by the fact that, while the Song of Songs is found in
the tripartite Bible's third section, identified as the Writings *(Kĕtûbîm)*,
it also belongs to another collection known as the *mĕgillôt* or scrolls.
The five biblical books in this collection were all read during the liturgy
on various feast days—the Song of Songs on the eighth day of Passover, Ruth during the Feast of Weeks (Pentecost), Lamentations on the
ninth day of Ab, Qoheleth (Ecclesiastes) during the Feast of Taberna-
cles, and Esther during Purim.

The Song of Songs enjoys other biblical connections. It is said of
Solomon that:

> He composed three thousand proverbs, and his songs *(šîr)* numbered a
> thousand and five. He would speak of trees, from the cedar that is in the
> Lebanon to the hyssop that grows in the wall; he would speak of ani-
> mals, birds, and reptiles, and fish (1 Kgs 4:32-33 [MT 5:12-13]).

Whether or not this claim is historically accurate, two elements of the
passage in particular are reminiscent of the Solomonic tradition. First,

the king is credited with composing lyric songs *(šîr)*. Second, the nature imagery mentioned is very similar to that found in the Song of Songs, and it exemplifies the tradition concerning Solomon's exceptional insight into human nature and natural phenomena. It is for this reason that the Song of Songs is read by many through the lens of Solomonic wisdom. We can conclude from the above that the poems that constitute the Song of Songs may have been secular in origin, but they have clear links with both the cultic and sapiential traditions of Israel, thus conferring religious significance on their erotic content.

Some believe that erotic poems such as these might easily come from a man who numbered among his wives "seven hundred princesses and three hundred concubines" (1 Kgs 11:3). However, in the ancient world, such marriages were based less on romantic interest than on political expediency. They cemented alliances with foreign kingdoms. Furthermore, the size of the harem was an indication of the wealth and power of the ruler. The character of Solomon's household was more a sign of his involvement in the affairs of state than of the heart. In fact, he may have had to allow foreign princesses into his kingdom because he was losing his status on the world scene, and such alliances would protect him from kingdoms that threatened him.

The earliest Jewish readings of the Song of Songs seem to have been literal, which led to its use as a drinking ditty. However, both the Jewish and the Christian groups soon employed an allegorical approach in its interpretation. This approach reflected aspects of the covenantal relationship between YHWH and Israel, or God and the Church. Such an interpretive approach lent itself to a spiritual understanding of the Song of Songs as found in writers of the Common Era, such as Philo of Alexandria and Maimonides.[3] A prominent Jewish method employed a kind of historical allegory that recounted Israel's story from its experience of the Exodus to the advent of the messiah (e.g., the Targum *Canticles Rabbah*[4]; the writings of the great Rashi and his grandson Rashbam[5]). A recent study even interprets the Song of Songs as a program intended to bring back Davidic rule after the exile.[6]

As early as Origen (ca. 240 C.E.), Christians began to read the book with devotional eyes that saw the relationship described there as one of spiritual marriage between God and the individual soul. This view was endorsed by such influential authors as Gregory of Nyssa, Jerome, Ambrose, Theodoret, and Cyril of Alexandria. It took on added signifi-

---

[3] See Pope, *Song of Songs*, 89–229; Murphy, *Song of Songs*, 11–41.

[4] Pope, *Song of Songs*, 93–6.

[5] Ibid., 102–3.

[6] Stadelmann, *Love and Politics*.

cance in the mysticism of the Middle Ages with the writings of Gregory the Great, William of Saint Thierry, Venerable Bede, Bernard of Clairvaux, as well as the sixteenth century writers Teresa of Avila and John of the Cross.[7] Spiritual interpretations of the Song of Songs usually include some form of allegory or typology. When allegory is employed, the nature imagery and the exchanges between the lovers are read as instances of double entendre, saying one thing but meaning another. In a typological approach, the book is read literally as an account of human love, but this love is seen as a type of the love that God has for humankind. The Christian allegory was either ecclesiological, which describes the relationship between Christ and the Church; tropological, which focuses on possible moral implications; or mariological, which views the Virgin Mary as the preeminent type of the Church. With the advent of critical scholarship, allegorical or typological interpretations have generally given way to literal readings, though various kinds of allegory are still widespread among Protestant evangelicals and found within some traditions of spiritual theology.

Several interpretations of the Song of Songs have been advanced, each one clearly dependent upon the literary classification to which the book is assigned. Aside from those which read the Song of Songs as an allegory, most of the interpretations can be classified in one of three other literary forms: a cultic reenactment, a dramatic performance, or a collection of love poems.

The ancient Near Eastern world produced various versions of a cultic reenactment of the death and rising of a fertility god. The two main characters in the Canaanite account are Ishtar, the moon goddess, and Tammuz, the sun god and the source of fertility. The absence of Tammuz sets Ishtar on a search for him that takes her to the netherworld. Finding him, she makes love to him and in that way she brings him back to life. His return signals the rebirth of nature. The abundance of foreign vocabulary in the Song of Songs and its rich nature imagery have reinforced the popularity of this ritualistic approach. Many believe that, though significantly reinterpreted, this cultic drama is the background for the Song of Songs.[8]

Two versions of a dramatic performance have been advanced. Some hold that there are two main characters, a Shulamite maiden and her shepherd love (Solomon), along with a chorus. Others maintain that the shepherd and the king are two different characters. In this theory, the drama unfolds in several acts, each determined by a change in location or the refrains recited by the chorus. Although there is very little

---

[7] Matter, *Voice of My Beloved*.

[8] For an explanation of this theory, see Pope, *Song of Songs*, 145–53.

story line, the Song of Songs does contain elements of conflict and resolution, and it celebrates the struggles and joys of human love.[9]

The allegorical, the liturgical, and the dramatic interpretations of the Song of Songs are all in some way imposed on the text from the outside. Still, each of these approaches reveals distinctive facets of the Song of Songs and opens up corresponding possibilities for understanding its message. However, critical scholarship has brought us back to a literal reading of the Song of Songs. The book is now regarded as a collection of love poetry, and it is usually interpreted as such. Its sensuous imagery and its depiction of an erotic affair celebrate the passion of heterosexual love. Three features set the Song of Songs apart from other biblical works. First, the sexuality within it is explicit and erotic, and it makes no excuses for this. Second, there is no mention of God in any of the poems. Third, while the focus of the Song of Songs is human behavior, it neither passes judgment on that behavior nor offers any moral teaching. These features may have contributed to its early allegorical interpretation, but such an interpretive approach is no longer promoted by scholars.

Even among those who regard the Song of Songs as a collection of love poems, views differ regarding its literary design and the number of poems which it comprises. While many commentators believe that the book is merely a collection of unrelated poems,[10] others, using various literary approaches, detect a certain literary unity within it.[11] In the final analysis, the designation of genre may come at least as much from the reader as from the text itself.[12]

Hebrew Poetry

It is very difficult to distinguish between prose and poetry in the Bible, because what have been identified as poetic features are present in both forms of literature.[13] The extent to which these features are used

---

[9] For an explanation of this theory, see Elliott, *Literary Unity*, 7–14.

[10] See Pope, *Song of Songs*, 54; Shea, "Chiastic Structure," 378–96; Tournay, *Word of God*, 32–40; Brenner, *Song of Songs*, 15; Falk, *Song of Songs*, 105; Snaith, *Song of Songs*, 6; Keel, *Song of Songs*, 17.

[11] See Rowley, "Interpretation," 212; Exum, "Literary and Structural Analysis," 47–79; Landy, *Paradoxes of Paradise*, 33–58; Carr, *Song of Solomon*, 45; Fox, *Song of Songs*, 194–5; Goulder, *Song of Fourteen Songs*, 2; Elliott, *Literary Unity*; Murphy, 65–6; Deckers, "Structure."

[12] Rowley, "Interpretation," 232.

[13] For an argument against the traditional distinction between prose and poetry see Kugel, *Idea of Biblical Poetry*, 85–7.

enables us to differentiate one form from the other. We are accustomed to think of poetry as speech organized in measured lines. However, Hebrew poetry contains characteristics that are quite different. In particular, it is noted for its terseness. Several features contribute to this. It uses very few connecting words, such as conjunctions; it is rich in parallelism, which paints pictures with swift, bold strokes; it employs ellipsis, the tendency to drop a major theme from the second part of a poetic line, expecting the reader to carry that theme over from the first line;[14] its imagery embodies multiple meanings in a concise form.

Biblical poetry is characterized by the regularity of its structure and by a particular technique known as parallelism. Unlike prose, which uses the sentence as its basic unit of expression, poetry is expressed in lines made up of short clauses called cola.[15] Most lines are bicola, with each colon containing three words. However, monocolon and tricolon lines are also found, as are cola with two or four words. One or more cola constitute a strophe, and one or more strophes constitute a stanza. It is basically this kind of structure that distinguishes poetry from other biblical forms of literature, such as narrative and law.

The question of poetic meter has been the subject of debate for centuries. Meter can be marked by the length of the syllable, by its accent, or by the pitch used in pronouncing it. Since no discernible pattern of meter has been discovered in those ancient Semitic languages closest to Hebrew, namely Akkadian and Ugaritic,[16] there is question whether or not it occurred in Hebrew poetry.[17] If it did, was the pattern a structural consideration based on counting syllables,[18] or metrical, based on stresses?[19] It is generally agreed that meter is a form of rhythm based on the repetition of sounds. In other words, rhythm can only be heard; it cannot be seen. The difficulty in assigning accent to written verse of an ancient language with no living native informants is obvious. Furthermore, those analysts who count accents do not always agree on which words are important enough to be considered. However, they ultimately agree that the most common pattern is a 3+3 line. Only in exceptional cases will this commentary address the question of meter.

---

[14] Ibid., 87–94; Watson, *Classical Hebrew Poetry*, 303–6.

[15] This unit is also called "stich" or "hemistich" by some commentators.

[16] Watson, *Classical Hebrew Poetry*, 91–7.

[17] The existence of any kind of meter is rejected by Kugel, *Idea of Biblical Poetry*, and by O'Connor, *Hebrew Verse Structure*.

[18] Freedman, "Acrostics and Metrics," 367–92.

[19] Alonso Schökel, *A Manual of Hebrew Poetics*, 34–47; Watson, *Classical Hebrew Poetry*, 97–113.

Parallelism, which is based on a kind of mathematical analogy, is a literary technique composed of couplets wherein the second clause of a colon or of a line corresponds more or less with the first. While this may be a helpful guide for classification, it is important to remember that the pattern itself originated in the field of mathematics and is not native to Hebrew poetry. Therefore, the poetry should not be forced to conform to it when it does not. Parallelism was initially further classified as synonymous—the second phrase merely repeats in different words the thought of the first; antithetical—the idea of the first is repeated in the second through the use of an antithesis; or synthetic or staircase—either an incomplete parallelism or one which contains the development in the second phrase of an idea from the first.[20]

While furthering the analysis of synonymy, repetition, and antithesis, recent scholarship has significantly altered these rather inadequate classifications of parallelism.[21] It now recognizes not only synonymy but also progression: the second line not only repeats the first, it adds something to it. Grammatical equivalence or contrast has come to be recognized as one of the basic characteristics of this poetic device. Such study includes both syntactic analysis (the study of the equivalence of one line with another) and morphological analysis (the study of the equivalence or contrast of the various elements of the line). The first classification includes parallelisms that are nominal/verbal, positive/negative, subject/object, or involve contrast in grammatical mood. The latter includes correspondences in person, gender, number, or definiteness.[22] The study of parallelism now recognizes four ways that the two phrases can be related: they can be interchangeable; the second can add to the meaning of the first; the second can be more important than the first; or the two phrases can comprise a unit.

As with all poetry, biblical verse employs various other poetic devices. Chief among them are simile and metaphor. The former is a comparison between two objects marked by the use of "as" or "like," while the latter suggests similarity where there is obvious disparity. Hyperbole, the deliberate use of exaggeration for the sake of effect, and personification, the assignment of human characteristics to inanimate objects, heighten the imaginative quality of verse. Hebrew poetry is noted for its play on sounds. In order to accomplish this it uses alliteration and assonance, the repetition of consonant and vowel sounds

[20] Lowth, *De sacra poesi Hebraeorum.*

[21] Kugel, *Idea of Biblical Poetry;* Berlin, *Dynamics of Biblical Parallelism;* Watson, *Traditional Techniques,* 104–261.

[22] Berlin, *Dynamics of Biblical Parallelism,* 31–63, 144–6; Watson, *Traditional Techniques,* 46; O'Connor, *Hebrew Verse Structure,* 87–136.

respectively; onomatopoeia, the imitation of the sound actually made by the referent; and paronomasia, a pun or play on words. Other poetic devices include enjambment, the run over of a sentence or clause from one colon to the next; chiasm, a pattern of the reversal in order of words or ideas; inclusion, the repetition of words or of a phrase at the beginning and the end of a poetic unit; and merism, polar word-pairs that include everything between the poles.

Probably the most significant poetic feature of the Song of Songs is its use of metaphor. Most metaphors compare two significantly different objects in order to uncover the presence of a particular characteristic that is obvious in one of them but not in the other. Every metaphor consists of three elements: the vehicle; the referent; and the tenor. The vehicle is the member of the comparison to which the characteristic naturally belongs. The referent is the other member, about which the comparison is made. The tenor (*tertium comparationis*) is the analogue, the actual characteristic of comparison. For example: "Your eyes are doves" (4:1). Here, a characteristic (the tenor of the metaphor) of the doves (the vehicle) is attributed to the eyes (the referent) of the woman. Some would say that the identified tenor is the gentle quality of the bird/the woman; others that it is the fluttering motion of the wings/ the eyelids.

The relationship between the vehicle and the referent may be representational. This means that a feature of one object represents a feature in an otherwise unrelated object. However, there is another way of understanding metaphor, a way that produces meaning by juxtaposition rather than comparison. In this second way, the relationship between the vehicle and the referent is presentational rather than representational. In this case, the association of ideas is based on emotional response rather than physical similarity. Here the poet is more intent on reproducing the emotional reaction to the charms of the woman than representing her physical beauty itself. Viewed from a presentational perspective, the metaphor "Your eyes are doves" generates a definite emotion, depending upon how the tenor is understood. When it denotes the gentleness of the bird, it can create a sense of delicate calm. When the reference is to fluttering wings/eyelids, a tantalizing excitement can be evoked.

The imagery found in the Song of Songs is as diverse as is the experience of love. Though most metaphors are drawn from familiar fauna and flora, others call on the arts, crafts and architecture, as well as the military realm. Some imagery is based on social position, while other images are derived from familial relationships. Several images appear to be more prominent than others; but a single image can be said to operate as the organizing principle of the entire collection, namely human passion. The erotic sentiments and the luxurious imagery of the Song of Songs find parallels in the love poetry from surrounding cultures, particularly Egyptian,[23] Akkadian and Ugaritic.[24] While there is not enough evidence to suggest any kind of literary dependence, the similarities cannot be denied.

The Song of Songs contains several examples of a particular kind of Arabic poem known as a *waṣf*.[25] This form of poem uses exaggerated metaphor and, in an orderly fashion, describes the body of the loved one, part by part. The imagery employed in such a poetic construction is normally taken from both nature and human creation. Most of the metaphors are visual allusions, but some of them appeal to other senses as well. While the imagery of the Song of Songs may seem strange—or even crude—to the modern reader, it must have been easily understood by the ancient Israelite and considered complimentary or it would not have become as popular as it was, nor would it have found its way into this collection of poetry.

Perhaps literary unity cannot be claimed on the basis of identical themes and imagery, since love poems generally share such characteristics. Nevertheless, there are certain characteristics that indicate significant homogeneity. Apparent is the repetition of words (e.g., my loved one, 1:13, 14, 16, etc.), phrases (e.g., like a gazelle, 2:9, 17; 8:14), and patterns that some have called refrains (e.g., I adjure you, O daughters of Jerusalem, 2:7; 3:5; 5:8; 8:4). Though the poems may have originated as discrete pieces, as they appear in this collection they create a kind of coherent plot of longing, searching, finding, losing, longing, etc. Furthermore, there is consistency in the characters' behavior. The interpretation of these stylistic features has resulted in great disparity among scholars in deciding on the number of poems present in the Song of Songs (the number ranges from five to fifty-two[26]) as well as the identity of the speaker. The following literary structure of six poetic units with a superscription has been adopted here: 1:1; 1:2–2:7; 2:8–3:5; 3:6–5:1; 5:2–6:3; 6:4–8:4; 8:5-14. This number is based on identification of both the speakers and the literary patterns. An explanation for this structuring follows.

---

[23] Fox's entire book *Song of Songs* is a comparison of these two collections.

[24] Pope quotes from studies that others have done in this area, *Song of Songs*, 54–89; Watson, *Classical Hebrew Poetry*, 4–10.

[25] Soulen, "The *waṣf*," 183–91; Fox, *Song of Songs*, 269–71; Falk, *Song of Songs*, 127–35.

[26] For a list of interpreters and the number of poems they isolate see Tournay, *Word of God*, 31.

The superscription (1:1) is clearly set off from the rest of the book. The first and second units (1:2–2:7; 2:8–3:5) are delineated by the same final solemn adjuration directed by the woman toward the daughters of Jerusalem (2:7; 3:5). The third unit (3:6–5:1), which begins with a poem that is clearly independent of what precedes it, is the man's praise of his loved one, while the fourth (5:2–6:3) is comparable praise of the man by the woman. The fifth unit (6:4–8:4) is delineated by the woman's solemn adjuration found earlier (8:4; compare 2:7; 3:5). What remains (8:5-14) seems to be a collection of disparate poems. The book will be examined with this structure in view.

Form critical study has provided certain genre classification that can assist us in understanding this rather complex literary creation. The material can be identified as poems of yearning (1:2-4; 2:6; 7:9b-10 [MT 7:10b-11]; 8:1-3), self-descriptions (1:5-6; 8:10), poems of admiration (1:9-17; 2:3; 4:9-15; 6:4-5a), accounts of some experience (2:8-10a; 3:1-5; 5:2-8; 6:11-12; 8:5b), characterizations of the physical charms of the loved one, similar to the Arabic *waṣf* (4:1-7; 5:10-16; 6:5b-7; 7:1-7 [MT 7:2-8]), and invitations to a tryst (2:10b-14; 4:8; 5:1; 7:11-13 [MT 7:12-14]).[27]

___

[27] For different classifications see Murphy, *Wisdom Literature*, 101–3; Fox, *Song of Songs*, 271–7.

COMMENTARY

SUPERSCRIPTION
(1:1)

The opening verse of the book, *šîr haššîrîm ʾăšer lîšlōmōh* (1:1), is an excellent example of alliteration. Some commentators also consider it an example of onomatopoeia, mimicking the actual sound of kissing.[1] As a superscription, it performs several significant functions: it identifies the book as a song *(šîr)*; it graces it with honorific prestige, identifying it as the "song of songs" *(šîr haššîrîm)*; and it affixes Solomonic authority to its message *(ʾăšer lîšlōmōh)*. This is a *šîr* or a lyric song, not a *mizmōr* or religious song. The singular form used here suggests that the editor who appended this superscription intended that, regardless of its original form and meaning, the collection in its final form should be regarded as a literary unit.[2]

The form, *šîr haššîrîm* (Song of Songs), is the Hebrew way of expressing the superlative. It sets this song apart from all other songs. Of all the lyric poems of the Bible, this particular one is the most sublime song, the song above all other songs. This designation is quite interesting when we remember that the Song of Songs is about passionate human love and not religious or political matters, as is the case with the biblical psalms. In other words, the lyric song that is erotic in nature is the one identified as being superior to all other songs.

This designation is followed by a modifying phrase *ʾăšer lîšlōmōh* (which is Solomon's). Since the preposition preceding Solomon's name can be translated in various ways, it could mean that authorship is ascribed to Solomon, or that the Song of Songs was dedicated to him, or that it was simply part of the royal holdings. Although he is explicitly mentioned six times in various poems (1:5; 3:7, 9, 11; 8:11, 12),

---

[1] Mariaselvam, *Song of Songs,* 64.
[2] *Contra* Keel, *Song of Songs,* 38–9.

Solomon himself plays no significant role in the drama portrayed. Instead, he seems to function as a symbol of wealth, a standard of comparison, or a fictitious way of according special honor to the man in the Song of Songs. The commentary that follows will show that the poems actually describe the woman's perspective in the love relationship and not the man's.[3] All of this suggests that the reference to Solomon should be understood as some kind of association with him rather than as an indication of actual authorship by him.

Most likely, the superscription confers Solomonic authority on the message of the book, in the same way as superscriptions confer such authority on many of the Proverbs (e.g., Prov 1:1; 10:1; 25:1) and even some of the psalms (e.g., Pss 72; 127). We might ask, Why would a collection of love lyrics be accorded Solomonic legitimation, if it had nothing to do with the man himself? Was this the only way for it to garner official approval within the religious community of Israel? Some commentators propose that the tradition about Solomon's many wives and concubines (see 1 Kgs 11:3) invited such an association. As interesting as it may be, this particular explanation only addresses a possible literary link between the tradition of the Judean king's romantic exploits and the passionate love depicted in these poems. It suggests *how* the book, with its erotic content, received approval; it does not explain *why* it was ultimately included in the list of sacred writings in the first place. We face today the same question that faced the rabbis at the time of Akiba: Why did the Song of Songs "defile the hands"?[4] However these issues are explained, the collection of love poems enjoys not only canonical status but also Solomonic legitimation. In other words, their message is considered authoritative wisdom.

This Solomonic legitimation places the Song of Songs in the category of ancient Israelite Wisdom Literature, alongside books like Job, Proverbs, Ecclesiastes, certain Psalms, Sirach, and the Wisdom of Solomon. The primary interest of that tradition is instruction in the proper ways of living. The sages were what we today would call humanists. Though religious people, they were concerned with human affairs and attentive to human welfare, values and dignity rather than

---

[3] Many commentaries identify the man as the lover (the active one in the relationship) and the woman as the beloved (the one receiving the love). Such designations not only reflect gender biases, but also are inaccurate representations of the character of the poems. Both the woman and the man are portrayed as passionate lovers and, therefore, each is also beloved to the other. In fact, it is the woman who is more prominent and the man who is the recipient of her passion.

[4] An expression that means "is sacred and requires washing one's hands both before and after touching it."

the things and activity of God. They taught that whatever benefited humankind was a good to be pursued, and whatever was harmful should be avoided and condemned. Their thinking was grounded in belief in an ordered creation, determined by God. They maintained that training of any kind, whether within the family, in the court, in the temple, or in preparation for a profession, was intended to impart the skills needed to succeed in that respective arena. The criterion for judging the value of any undertaking was the degree of well-being or success that it provided, well-being or success that flowed naturally from the order placed in creation by the creator.

The wisdom teachers did not advocate the pursuit of happiness for its own sake. Happiness or success was considered a by-product of an upright life, a life lived in harmony with the order set by God. Since the sages regarded well-being and happiness as evidence that one's life and behavior were in accord with this order, success was considered concrete evidence of the wisdom or righteousness of the person who succeeded. What the sages actually counseled was upright living, and they usually had very definite lessons to teach about cosmic, familial or civic order. These lessons were learnt from the experiences of life, experience that revealed how the world worked. Though descriptive in themselves, they contained a final teaching, similar to the popular saying "and the moral of the story is. . . ."

Although the wise women and men believed that there was a proper way of behaving, they did not insist on a rigid standard that would fit every circumstance. They acknowledged that varying circumstances made each case unique. In fact, only those who were able to evaluate the situation and decide on the best course of action were considered wise. The truly sagacious person was the one who could draw on a store of wisdom gained from personal experience, social custom or religious tradition, and then would choose a course of action that seemed to fit the situation. Placing the Song of Songs within the Wisdom tradition makes a bold claim. For it to be wisdom teaching, it must be more than a report of the romantic escapades of the king. It must contain insights beneficial for right living, insights that will enhance human life. A careful examination of these erotic poems will illuminate some of the lessons it has to teach.

MUTUAL YEARNING
(1:2–2:7)

The first poetic unit of the Song of Songs (1:2–2:7) consists of a lyric poem spoken by the woman (1:2-6) and a series of poems wherein the couple individually proclaim their admiration for each other (1:7–2:7). The shift between second- and third-person pronouns utilized here (1:2) has been the source of much confusion. Although some consider this shift as evidence of a change in the direction of the address or the one speaking, most scholars today recognize it as a simple poetic device, called *enallagē*. This technique, which is found quite frequently in the poetry of the ancient world, is obvious in Psalm 23:

> ¹The LORD is my shepherd, I shall not want.
> ²He makes me lie down in green pastures;
> he leads me beside still waters;
> ³he restores my soul.
> He leads me in right paths
> for his name's sake.
> ⁴Even though I walk through the darkest valley,
> I fear no evil;
> for you are with me;
> your rod and your staff—
> they comfort me.
> ⁵You prepare a table before me
> in the presence of my enemies;
> you anoint my head with oil;
> my cup overflows.
> ⁶Surely goodness and mercy shall follow me
> all the days of my life,
> and I shall dwell in the house of the LORD
> my whole life long.

There we see that verses 1-3 speak about God in the third person; verses 4-5 are second-person direct address, speaking to God; verse 6 is third-person description again. Understanding this literary feature resolves the confusion caused by the change of voice at several points in the poem.

Love Better Than Wine: 1:2-6

The first lyric poem ascribed to the woman can be further divided into two segments: a romantic soliloquy wherein she fantasizes about her lover[1] (vv. 2-4); and a discourse directed to the daughters of Jerusalem (vv. 5-6). Various linguistic patterns can be found in each of these segments as well. The soliloquy contains two word-patterns: "your lovemaking more than wine" and "they love you." The woman proclaims to the man that she values "your lovemaking more than wine" (vv. 2, 4).[2] The phrase can function as a refrain, connected to and bringing to completion the preceding idea. However, in the first instance of this word-pattern, the phrase is part of another discernible pattern, a chiastic structure (vv. 2b-3a):

A   good

B   your lovemaking

C   wine

C'   scent

B'   ointments

A'   good

Only by forcing an interpretation of the text can one detect a similar chiastic pattern in the second instance of this word-pattern (v. 4cd).[3] With the second word-pattern in the soliloquy, the woman assures the man that "they love you" (vv. 3, 4). In Hebrew this is one word (ʾăhēbûkā), and in each case of its appearance it is the last word of a tricolon. Taken

---

[1] The use of "lover" and "beloved" will not designate gender, but the act of loving. When the woman is the one doing the loving, she will be referred to as the lover and the man as the beloved, and vice versa.

[2] Author's translation, explained below.

[3] Goulder posits a second chiasm in verse 4c and 4d: "We shall speak of your loves more than wine, more than handsome men they love you" (*Song of Fourteen Songs*, 12).

separately, each word-pattern structures the poetry in a particular way. However, taken together they preclude such discrete structuring and suggest, instead, the overlapping of various linguistic patterns.

The woman's soliloquy expresses her ardent yearning. Everything about this poem is exquisite in its artistry. The metaphors used appeal to taste and smell. They engender an experience of intoxication and a sense of extravagance. Furthermore, the sensuous character of the imagery is reinforced by the very structure of the cola. A careful examination will demonstrate this. The importance of the phrase "your lovemaking more than wine" has already been stated. A look at its composition will confirm this claim. First, the opening verb *yiššāqēnî* (let him kiss me) is remarkably similar to *yašqēnî* (let him give me drink). This paronomasia (play on words) both identifies the form of kissing and supports the relationship metaphorically drawn between kissing and drinking wine.

The custom of nose kissing was quite common in the ancient Near East. However, the choice of verbs and the metaphors used indicate that the woman is asking for mouth kissing. An examination of the metaphor will reveal this: wine is the vehicle of meaning; kissing is the referent receiving the meaning; intoxication is the tenor or point of comparison. The metaphor functions in a presentational manner, evoking intense emotional response. The woman yearns for the kind of deep mouth kissing that is intoxicating, that sends a thrill through the body similar to the sensation brought on by strong wine. The metaphor can be taken a step further. Besides a sense of intoxication, it also suggests vulnerability and trust. Since the mouth is a primary gateway to the physical interior of the person, passionate open-mouth kissing literally opens the lovers to each other. It suggests a willingness to take another into oneself and to make that other one's own, as well as the desire to enter into the other and lose oneself within that other. Only unfeigned trust can dispose one to such vulnerability. From the outset, the Song of Songs paints a picture of human passion at its best, mutually trusting and open to the other in unguarded love.

The paronomasia may link kissing and wine, but it is clear that such a metaphoric relationship is not one of congruence. The structure of the phrase shows us that the man's lovemaking is clearly better than wine (vv. 2, 4). The word for love *(dôdîm)* is plural, referring to more than one romantic act. Thus "lovemaking" is a better rendering of the word than simply "love." Hebrew possesses no explicit forms for the comparative or superlative adjectival expression. We have already seen an example of the superlative form in the superscription (Song of Songs). The comparative form is usually expressed periphrastically by prefixing the preposition *min* (from) to the inferior element in the comparison. Here *min* is the prefix of "wine," indicating that the inebriating effect of wine is inferior to the exhilaration awakened in the woman by the man's lovemaking.

This opening appeal made by the woman lays bare the unabashed ardor of her desire. This is not a woman who is fantasizing about what lovemaking might be like. She has already experienced it; she knows its excitement; she has been thrilled by the intoxication of her lover's deep kisses; and she wants more. Too often the sexual yearnings and the sense of passionate exhilaration of women have either been denied, or minimized as insignificant, or condemned as inappropriate. There is none of that groundless chauvinistic bias in this opening proclamation. This woman is a vital, passionate, sensual person with powerful sexual desires and single-minded determination to satisfy them. The creative expressions that she uses to describe the lovemaking of her lover are as provocative as the erotic experience itself is driven by desire. This is no shrinking violet, hidden away in the corner of the garden. Rather, she is in the full flower of her womanhood, and she is indulging herself in it. Furthermore, while genuine lovemaking is certainly an experience of mutual arousal, in this particular poem, it is the woman who is preoccupied with the way her lover can excite her, not how she can please him.

A second paronomasia (v. 3) is found in the play on the sounds of the words for "oil" (*šemen*) and "name" (*šem*). Here again, the poetic structure supports the meaning of the metaphor. In the ancient world, one's name was considered the very essence of one's personality. That is the meaning intended here. Examining the metaphor we see that the man's name/person (the referent of the metaphor) is considered fragrant (the tenor), like anointing oil (the vehicle). Some interpreters argue that the *min* comparative prefix found in the previous colon (better than wine) functions in this colon as well. If this is the case, it means that the man's name is considered more fragrant than anointing oil. Either interpretation would be acceptable.

In addition to the fragrance explicitly intended by the metaphor, the vehicle carries other characteristics that can be applied to the referent (the man). For example, the best ointments are rare and usually quite costly. When related to the man, these features heighten his uniqueness in the eyes of his lover. This would suggest that he is rare among men and of great value. Furthermore, he has so filled her senses that, like a fragrant bouquet, his charms permeate his surroundings and remain in the air even when he has departed. Finally, his desirability is definitely not a figment of the woman's imagination, as is so often the case when one falls in love. This man seems to be everything that she claims he is, for other young women are enamored of him as well.

In this initial soliloquy, the imagery the woman uses to describe her desire is vividly sensuous. It appeals to both taste and smell, the sensations of which not only are heady but frequently coalesce, creating a rich and multifaceted sensation that is very difficult to analyze precisely. The woman yearns to be intoxicated by the taste of the man's lovemaking and to be overcome by the aroma of his provocative being. Her desire for him is tangible. She can taste it; she can smell it.

With the exception of the final colon (v. 4e), the verbs in verse 4 are all dynamic: draw, run, brought, exult and rejoice, exult. The energetic images that they paint create more of a collage than a single scene. There is urgency in the woman's entreaty: she pleads to be drawn to the man. Her passionate petition seems to be granted and she is brought into his chambers. There is a suggestion of union, which results in rejoicing. The first two verbs in this series imply that while she has been speaking to the man, he has not been actually present to her. Perhaps she has been in a kind of reverie, absorbed in thoughts of him. Now she implores that he take her to himself. Her request appears to be answered, if not in fact, as least in her reverie. She is brought into his chambers (*ḥeder*),[4] a place that affords the kind of privacy that lovers seek. Here we see one of the underlying themes of the entire book: the movement from absence to presence to absence again and then to presence, the longing for union and the consummation of desire only to yearn once more.

Mention of the king has resulted in various interpretations. Some commentators consider this a reference to Solomon, and they identify the man of the Song of Songs with the Judean king. Others believe that a third character has been introduced into the poetry. Actually, the reference is probably a term of endearment that is frequently associated with situations of love. In Akkadian love literature, lovers are often accorded royal titles.[5] Lovers themselves use such exalted terms to speak about their loved ones. In line with this, society also grants them the benefits of such a royal fiction. Some societies even dress the bride and groom in royal finery and pay them appropriate homage during the wedding celebration. This royal motif allows us to consider the anointing oils mentioned in the previous verse as part of royal accouterment, even though they are still understood metaphorically. Mention of the king's chambers introduces a theme that appears several times in the Song of Songs (see 2:4; 3:4; 8:2), a theme that implies both intimacy and extravagance.

---

[4] The room of the bridegroom (Joel 2:16), the place where Samson planned to meet his wife (Judg 15:1).

[5] See Botterweck and Ringgren, eds., *Theological Dictionary*, 3:148–9; Munro, *Spikenard and Saffron*, 35–42.

The change in pronominal form *(enallagē)* has generated various interpretations of verse 4. To whom does the woman refer when she says, "We will exult and rejoice in you"? Is "we" a reference to herself and the man she loves? Or to herself and the maidens that are mentioned earlier? The next colon indicates that it is the man's lovemaking that is being extolled, and who other than the man and the woman would have knowledge of his romantic behavior? Consequently, "we" must refer to the lovers themselves. The translation of the final colon of the verse complicates the interpretation even further.[6] The favored rendering is, "Rightly do they love you." Referring to the final word of verse 3, "they" is a reference to the maidens. Even though only the woman has intimate knowledge of the man's romantic character, his charms are recognized by others, and these others can see how he has captured her imagination and her heart. It is not inappropriate to say that "they love you."

The desirability of the man has been established. Not only the central protagonist of the Song of Songs but other women as well are captivated by his charms. Once again the character of the women portrayed here belies certain sexual stereotypes. These women are not primarily interested in making themselves attractive to the man. Rather, they are occupied with the man's attractiveness. This is particularly true with regard to the central woman. Although he is the one who takes her to himself, it is she who initiates this rendezvous; she asks him to draw her to himself, and he acquiesces to her desire. This is not to suggest that he himself is disinterested, for the lovemaking that is being extolled is his. Instead, it is clear that the desire and passion are shared by both the woman and the man.

The second segment of this first lyric poem ascribed to the woman is a self-descriptive discourse directed to the daughters of Jerusalem (vv. 5-6). The identity of these women is not clear. They may simply be residents of the city who are directly involved only with the woman and not with the man. From a literary point of view, they act as a kind of foil for her. It is to them that she expresses any negative sentiments she might experience or any reservations she might harbor regarding certain aspects of the circumstances within which she finds herself. She is most likely addressing them when it is clear that she is not speaking to the man. They pose questions (see 3:6; 5:9; 6:1) to which she provides answers, thus facilitating the forward movement of the dialogue.

Several clearly defined poetic techniques are woven together in this poem. There is an example of parallelism:

[6] The Hebrew *mêšārîm* has been translated "rightly," "righteous ones," or "smooth" (a description of the wine).

a   like

b   the tents of Kedar

a'   like

b'   the curtains of Solomon

and of chiasm:

a   I am black and beautiful (O daughters of Jerusalem)

b   like the tents of Kedar

b'   like the curtains of Solomon

a'   I am blackish [NRSV: "dark"]

There are also wordplays on the words "black," "gaze on," and "vineyard." As with the previous poem, these techniques overlap, making any identification of a definite structure quite tentative.

Speaking to the daughters of Jerusalem, the woman unabashedly attests to her own comeliness; she is black and beautiful. The text indicates that her dark complexion is the result of exposure to the sun rather than dark skin pigmentation, which is a specific racial feature.[7] Still there appears to be some sort of discrimination regarding her coloring, perhaps a class bias, for the woman seems to be defending her dark complexion. Unlike the sheltered women of the elite (the daughters of Jerusalem?), lower class women were required to work outdoors, subjecting themselves to the harshness of the elements. This does not necessarily mean that the woman in the Song of Songs was from the lower classes. It simply attempts to explain any social bias against dark skin. The Hebrew conjunction *wĕ* can yield the simple connective "and" or the adversative "but." Traditionally this verse has been translated with the adversative, "black *but* beautiful," a rendering that suggests blackness is not beautiful, but there is an exception in the case of this woman. Such a translation shows that a color preference that may have originated as a class bias has lingered in various interpretations, justifying and reinforcing racial prejudice. In this passage, the woman may explain her dark complexion, but she clearly does not believe that it detracts from her beauty or her desirability in the eyes of her beloved. On the contrary, the similes she employs to characterize her complexion accentuate the merit of blackness.

The woman uses two similes in parallel construction:

---

[7] *Contra* Copher, "Black Presence," 149.

a   like the tents

b   of Kedar

a'   like the curtains

b'   of Solomon

She first compares her coloring to the goat-haired nomadic tents of
Kedar, the tribe that sprang from Ishmael (see Gen 25:13), a tribe that
eventually came to be known for its opulence (see Jer 49:28; Ezek
27:21). The mention of this tribe is an example of poetic artistry. It calls
to mind the wealth with which it is associated, and its name constitutes
a simple word play on one of the Hebrew words for "black" (*qādar*).
The second metaphor compares the woman's coloring with the curtains of Solomon. This colon can be interpreted in different ways. *Šlm* is
the root from which come both *šĕlōmōh* (Solomon) and *šalmāh*, a south
Arabian nomadic tribe.[8] In fact, in the original Hebrew text, which contained only consonants, *šĕlōmōh* and *šalmāh* would be identical. Some
commentators adopt the second reading instead of the first. This reading would strengthen the parallelism (Kedar/Salmah), because both
were nomadic tribes. However, while such change may strengthen the
linguistic character of the parallelism, it can also weaken its semantic
force. The extravagance associated with the court of Solomon is an important theme in these poems.

Association with the Judean king furthers the royal motif so prevalent in the Song of Songs and reinforces the idea of beauty. The curtains
recall the tapestries that hung in the wilderness tabernacle (see Exod
26:1-13; 36:8-17) and that, though not attested to by biblical evidence,
most likely adorned the temple of Solomon. Finally, litters of the kind
mentioned later in the Song of Songs and ascribed to Solomon (3:7, 9)
were also outfitted with curtains meant to conceal the identity of the
occupants and to shield them from inclement elements. These two
similes are employed as evidence that dark coloring does not always
denote inferiority. In fact, sometimes, as in this case, it denotes great
wealth.

The woman herself may be unapologetic regarding her coloring,
but it appears to have been the object of the scrutiny of others. The first
two cola boast two quite distinctive poetic techniques, a paronomasia
and an alliteration. Playing on the words for "gaze," the woman asks
that the daughters of Jerusalem not gaze on her with disdain because
the sun, here personified, has gazed on her with the force of its burning
rays. It is precisely this gaze that has darkened her skin. The alliteration

[8] Pope, *Song of Songs*, 320.

is striking (ʾal-tirʾûnî šeʾănî šĕḥarḥōret / šeššĕzāpatnî haššāmeš; "Do not gaze at me because I am black [NRSV "dark"]; because the sun has gazed on me"). The repeated "s" sounds suggest the sizzling sound of something cooking. The heat of the sun has actually cooked her skin.

In this self-affirmation of the woman, the various meanings of the word "vineyard" move the poem from an explanation of her coloring to a reference to presumed sexual irresponsibility on her part, the probable reason for her brothers' outrage. The vineyard theme is rich in meaning. On the literal level, it represents one of the most common and most profitable occupations of the Near East. The grapes and raisins that a vineyard yields and the wine produced from its fruit are staples of the diet of the people in this part of the world. For this reason, the vine became a symbol of basic sustenance (see 1 Kgs 4:25 [MT 5:5]; 2 Kgs 18:31; Mic 4:4) and even of prosperity (see Deut 8:8). The woman is said to have been made keeper of the vineyards. This would explain her exposure to the sun and the subsequent tanning of her skin. On a more figurative level, the vineyard and its fruitfulness are known to have represented people. Perhaps the most familiar example of this is found in the famous poem in Isa 5:1-7, where the loved one (Israel) is metaphorically depicted as a vineyard that was lovingly tended. Despite this, it still produced wild grapes. The fruitfulness of the vine has also served as a metaphor for female sexual fecundity (see Ps 128:3; Ezek 19:10).[9] It is in this latter sense that it is used in the Song of Songs as well.

The ownership of the vineyards is not mentioned here. The fact that the brothers assigned the woman to oversee the first vineyard indicates that they exercised some form of authority over it, and also over her and her life. Their anger with her could be connected with her negligence in properly attending to the second vineyard, which is identified as belonging to her. While it is true that women did on occasion claim ownership of land, it was only when there was no legitimate male heir and such an exception was considered necessary in order to assure that the land not be lost to the family inheritance (see Josh 17:3-6). Such a situation was not the case here. The woman had male siblings who would inherit; they are precisely the ones who put her in charge of the vineyards. While the first mention of vineyard (v. 6d) should probably be understood literally, in the second reference and elsewhere in the Song of Songs (8:12) vineyard appears to be a symbol of the woman's sexuality.[10]

[9] Munro, *Spikenard and Saffron*, 99.

[10] See Pope, *Song of Songs*, 326–8; Fox, *Song of Songs*, 102; Falk, *Song of Songs*, 155; Murphy, *Song of Songs*, 128; Bloch and Bloch, *Song of Songs*, 141.

Nowhere in the book is there a reference to her father.[11] Her brothers seem to have assumed responsibility for her (1:6; 8:8), a practice quite common in patriarchal societies. While no father is mentioned in these poems, reference to a mother is found in several places (see 3:4, 11; 6:9; 8:1, 2, 5). Here the phrase "my mother's sons" suggests full rather than half brothers, children of the same mother with whom the woman should be able to enjoy a special closeness. This closeness is most likely one springing from kinship rather than mere emotional attachment. It may be this very bond of kinship that explains their protective attitude toward her, a protectiveness that she spurns.

There is irony in the mutual play between various meanings of "gaze" and "black" and "vineyard." The woman is appointed to oversee the vineyard. This out-of-doors responsibility exposes her to the gaze of the sun, which darkens her skin. She implores the daughters of Jerusalem not to gaze with disdain at her darkness. Her brothers are already displeased with her because she did not properly supervise her own vineyard, her own self, suggesting some illicit sexual liaison. It is not clear whether or not the couple ever really consummate their love. While there is no explicit mention of coitus, many of the double entendres suggest that such an understanding is intended. The reference to the woman's vineyard is one such instance.

The contrast between the sentiments expressed in the two segments of this lyric poem alerts us to some of the struggles that the woman faces. On the one hand, she is enraptured by her lover and fantasizes about making love with him. On the other hand, she encounters criticism from both family members and citizens of the city. These two realities set up a challenging dilemma. If she pursues her amorous obsession, she will risk being discovered and subjected to even further reproach. However, the kind of passion that has consumed her tends to be reckless, free of restraint and oblivious to danger. The tension that we find in the very first poem in this collection is present throughout the entire Song of Songs. It actually highlights the depths of love that the woman possesses and the lengths to which she will go in order to enjoy it. Clearly, hers is an all-encompassing love.

---

[11] For imagery characterizing family life see Munro, *Spikenard and Saffron*, 69–79. According to this understanding, Landy's argument that the father is represented by phallic symbols seems to be an unnecessary assertion. Phallic symbols are part of the characterization of the male lover. The absence of the father is viewed here as but another aspect of the female dominance in the poems. See Landy, *Paradoxes of Paradise*.

A Beloved beyond Compare: 1:7–2:7

Both the scene and the sentiments change abruptly. Here we come upon the lovers themselves. We overhear their exchanges of tenderness (1:7-11, 15-17) and their rhapsodic monologues (1:12-14; 2:1-7). These are poems of mutual admiration and passionate yearning. They are the kind that lovers proclaim in intimate privacy; they are not normally meant for the ears of others. The setting itself moves first from the vineyard to the fields of the shepherds (vv. 7-8), then to the world of the pharaoh (vv. 9-11), and finally to a trysting place of intoxication (2:4-6). The imagery that describes the couple's desire for and their enjoyment of each other corresponds to the respective setting in which they are found.

As is usually the case, it is the woman who speaks. She initiates the dialogue; it is her longing that orchestrates the movement of the poems. She addresses the man as the one "whom my soul loves" (1:7; compare 3:1, 2, 3, 4). Although the Hebrew *nepeš* does not yield exactly the same meaning as does the Greek *psychē*, both words refer to the whole person and, though they are generally translated "soul," they are also translated as "life." The difference between these two words lies in their nuances. The Greek word implies a spiritual dimension. The Hebrew, being a much more concrete language, suggests a kind of physical yet somewhat nonmaterial source of life, namely, the breath. Used here the phrase implies that the woman loves this man with the very source of her life,[12] and she is conscious of this love with every breath that she draws.

The play on both the sound and the meaning of the woman's words captures her desire and the predicament in which it places her. She addresses her lover with a double imperative: "Tell me . . . where!" "Where do you pasture?" "Where do you cause to lie down?" In the Hebrew text neither of these verbs has an object, and the ambiguity of this construction opens the questions to double entendre. In the first query, the verb could mean either "where do you pasture your flock?" or "where do you eat?" The first option is a simple question about location. The second option has sexual connotations, and the question it poses is ultimately answered in later poems (see 2:16; 6:3). The causative form of the second verb indicates that the shepherd causes something other than himself to lie down, presumably his flock. This rendering supports the idea that the woman is here asking where he pastures his flock, where he has them lie down to rest at noontime during the heat of the day. Most likely she has in mind a rendezvous with

---

[12] Deckers, "Structure," 189–92.

him, and she asks for information about this place so that she does not
have to wander from pasture to pasture looking for him.

The word for "covering" or "veil" (ʿōṭĕyâ) is obscure, and its meaning continues to be disputed. It is very close in sound to the verb that is
translated "go astray" (ṭōʿăyâ), thus reinforcing the idea of wandering
about. She states that if she must go in search of her lover, she will
cover herself in order to hide her identity from his companions. The
reason for such disguise is not given. It is certainly not because she is
ashamed of the love that they share, for she unabashedly proclaims it
elsewhere. Perhaps the presence of an unaccompanied woman, one
who is not a member of the band of shepherds, would cast a cloud of
suspicion on the moral integrity of their love, and she certainly would
not want it to be misunderstood. Some believe that this veil suggests
the covering of prostitutes who often frequented the fields seeking a
liaison. While such a disguise could put the woman at risk, it would
probably not jeopardize the man's position, because such encounters
were quite common in certain societies. Whatever the case may be, the
intensity of her yearning is such that she is willing to take this risk in
order to meet him in the fields.

There is a mocking tone to the man's reply. The verb form suggests:
"If you do not know, you should have known." There is no rancor in
this response, just a tease, for he calls her "the fairest among women,"[13]
and then directs her to the place where he can be found. Just as she initially described him as a shepherd, so he refers to her as one who shepherds young goats (gĕdîyôt). This pastoral motif might be as much a
metaphoric ploy as is the royal fiction that appears so often in the Song
of Songs. The bucolic character of shepherding bespeaks peace and a
life governed by the movements of nature, themes that are prominent
in these poems. This motif explains both the regular presence of the
lovers in the fields and the frequent mention of flocks. In this instance
"goats" carries a double meaning. The common form of the word is
gĕdî. Because this word appears in parallel construction with breasts in
a later poem (see 1:13-14), some believe that it carries that same meaning here. This rendering is further strengthened by the fact that the
woman's breasts are later characterized as twin fawns of the gazelle
(4:5; 7:3 [MT 7:4]).

The man continues speaking with a song of admiration that praises
his lover's sexual attractiveness as well as the enhancement of her
beauty that jewelry provides (vv. 9-11). The poem, which consists of

[13] Because this expression is used elsewhere by the daughters of Jerusalem (5:9;
6:1), some think that they are speaking here as well. See Goulder, *Song of Fourteen
Songs*, 13; Elliott, *Literary Unity*, 52–4; Keel, *Song of Songs*, 53.

three verses composed of six cola, moves from the longing and searching of the woman to the adulation of the man. He calls her "my friend" *(raʿyātî)*, a special term of endearment applied only to women and used by him quite consistently (see 1:15; 2:2, 10, 13; 4:1; 5:2; 6:4). The masculine form of the word *(rēʿî)* is found in parallel construction with "beloved" (5:16). This accounts for its often being translated "my love," as is the case here. The term echoes the sound of the words for "pasture" and "shepherd" (vv. 7-8), thus linking this image with the themes that preceded it.

In the first verse of this poem of admiration, the man compares the woman to a mare let loose among the stallions of the pharaoh's chariotry. The tantalizing presence of the mare was able to throw those otherwise well-disciplined horses into total confusion and disarray. Such a comparison may seem foreign and even offensive to contemporary sensitivities, but the meaning conveyed by the imagery is quite striking. The equine frenzy that it suggests aptly illustrates the man's perception of the sexual irresistibility of the woman he loves. The metaphor implies that her charms are able to unsettle even the most disciplined of men. Her mere presence can cause them to lose control of themselves.

In the second and third verses, a second dimension of the metaphor is employed. It shifts the point of comparison from the mare's seductiveness to its extraordinary adornment. The bridles of the horses of royalty were often extravagantly decorated with colorful tassels, fringes and trappings of ivory or precious metal. Just as this finery added to the horses' grandeur, so the jewelry that the woman wears on her face and around her neck complements her own natural attractiveness. The exact nature of this jewelry is not stated, but the bridle metaphor suggests that the reference might be to dangling earrings or nose rings and necklaces consisting of several rows or strands of ornate stones. Earlier the woman had proclaimed that her dark coloring did not detract from her being beautiful *(nāʾweh)*. Now her lover affirms that she is indeed beautiful *(nāʾweh)*. In fact, he considers her the fairest among women. This is the kind of romantic adulation engaged in by lovers of all times. Even superlatives are inadequate to describe the allurements of the beloved.

The exchange of sentiments continues in the next verses, although the woman does not respond directly to the man. Her song of admiration (vv. 12-14) is more a love-monologue. She rhapsodizes about the majesty she perceives in him and the pleasure that she takes in him. Her song balances the three-verse, six-cola structure of the previous poem. It also resembles its thematic structure: the first verse states the fundamental theme and the next two verses develop that theme in greater detail. The unifying theme in this poem is the man's intoxicating fragrance. It is elaborated in the second and third verses of the poem by means of metaphors that are in parallel construction. This poem contains the first appearance of the epithet most frequently used by the woman in reference to the man—"my love" *(dôdî)*. Some form of this Hebrew word is found thirty-three times in the Song of Songs and only in reference to the man. An Akkadian equivalent of the word for "love" or "darling," also reserved for men, occasionally appears in the literature of that culture as part of a royal epithet.[14] The use of this word with the nuances found in Akkadian literature might help to explain some of the other references and allusions to royalty that are found in the Song of Songs (1:4, 12, 17; 3:6-11; 7:1, 5 [MT 7:2, 6]).

The couch on which the king reclines is the kind that could be used for either eating or lovemaking. Its use here is open for either interpretation, thus strengthening the link between these two very sensual activities. The metaphors that follow leave no question as to the sexual meaning intended here. Nard, a fragrant ointment found in the region of India, often acted as a love-charm. The fact that it was rare only added to its singular value. As an allusion to the fragrance of the woman,[15] it suggests sexual arousal as well as the kind of fascination that is inspired by what is out of the ordinary. In the picture drawn here, the man is reclining on a couch, prepared for love, and is enveloped by the exotic scent of his lover's allurement.

Just as the woman is the source of her lover's pleasure, so he is the source of hers. As mentioned above, the second and third verses of this poem are in parallel construction:

a   bag of myrrh

b   my love to me

c   that lies between my breasts

a'   cluster of henna

b'   my love to me

c'   in the vineyards of En-gedi

Myrrh and henna are two exotic perfumes that were highly valued in the ancient Near East. Myrrh, imported from Arabia and India, was a

---

[14] Botterweck and Ringgren, eds. *Theological Dictionary,* 3:148–9.

[15] Some commentators maintain that the reference is to the scent of the man, in line with the metaphors that follow. See Elliott, *Literary Unity,* 57–8; Fox, *Song of Songs,* 105.

spicy gum resin of certain trees. It served as a perfume for clothing and sometimes as a medicine. It was also used to anoint priests and ritual vessels and so was considered a sacred oil as well. Thus myrrh connotes intoxication, healing, and holiness. The henna shrub with its roselike flowers flourished in Egypt and Palestine. Apparently it grew at En-gedi (literally translated "spring of the kid"), a flourishing oasis located in a ravine in the wilderness on the western shore of the Dead Sea. The vibrant presence of this shrub in the midst of the barren desert is an apt metaphor of the uniqueness of this deeply loved man.

There is literary evidence that Jewish women wore sachets of spices between their breasts.[16] Comparing her lover to such a bag of myrrh suggests that that is precisely where he is resting. If En-gedi is also a reference to her breasts (v. 8) and, as seen earlier, if vineyard is an allusion to the sexuality of the woman herself (v. 6), then the second metaphor of this parallel construction suggests the same image. It is not that the man is wearing rare and intoxicating perfumes; he himself *is* the rare and intoxicating fragrance (v. 3). The imagery of this poem implies that the woman and the man are enraptured with each other as heady aromas intoxicate those who breathe in the air that they fill. The form of the verb translated "rest" suggests a long period of time. Here it might imply the entire night. This is not a description of a brief encounter, but of a long and passionate embrace.

The dialogue of mutual admiration continues with a brief exchange expressed in a kind of parallel fashion (vv. 15-17). Gazing at each other the lovers cry out, first the man:

(v. 15a)

    a   Ah,

    b   you are beautiful

    c   my love *(raʿyātî)*

and then the woman:

(v. 16a)

    a'   Ah,

    b'   you are beautiful

    c'   my love *(dôdî)*

In his cry, the man repeats his exclamation, "you are beautiful!" This is the term of endearment he uses most frequently to describe his lover

---

[16] Mishnah *Sabbath* 6.3.

(1:8; 2:10, 13; 4:1, 7, 10; 5:9; 6:1, 4, 10; 7:1, 6 [MT 7:2, 7]). His attention is caught by the dovelike quality of her eyes. There is nothing in the text to suggest which quality of the dove is the precise tenor of this metaphor. Is it the dove's soft oval shape? Its pure color? The gentle motion of its wings that resemble the fluttering eyelashes of a shy or coquettish maiden? The delicacy of the bird? Doves are commonly depicted as messengers of love. Are the woman's glances communicating a desire for romance? Rather than decide on one feature as the possible tenor of the metaphor, it is probably better to retain the ambiguity of the reference, thus respecting the polyvalent possibilities of the image.

It is next the woman's turn to acclaim the beauty of her lover. It is clear that his attractiveness is every bit as seductive to her as hers is to him. When he spoke, he repeated his acclamation "You are beautiful!" She uses a slightly different expression to reinforce her praise: "truly lovely!" She continues in her praise, speaking for both of them. The threefold repetition of plural possessives suggests mutual sharing, not necessarily ownership. The clauses can be laid out in parallel fashion:

a　　our couch

b　　　　green

a'　　beams (of our house)

b'　　　　cedar

a"　　our rafters

b"　　　　pine

As clear as this structure may be, it does not aid in determining the nature of the couple's trysting place. Is this a description of an elaborately constructed room of cedar and pine, a room that contains a couch on which are strewn newly cut branches? Such a depiction would certainly coincide with the royal allusion prominent in the preceding poem. Or is this a love nest in the forest, a place where lovers frequently retired for the privacy that their lovemaking required? Whether the place of rendezvous is a luxurious room or a luxuriant spot in the woods, the resplendence of its character corresponds to the magnificence of the loving encounter that occurs within it.

The imagery of the next three verses is vernal. Characteristics of flowers and fruit trees are applied first to the woman (2:1-2) and then to the man (v. 3). In parallel fashion, he declares that she is :

a　　a rose

b　　　　of Sharon

a'   a lily

b'   of the valleys

The exact horticultural classification of the flowers traditionally translated as "rose" and "lily" is difficult to determine. What is translated "rose" could be a crocus, a narcissus, a meadow saffron, even a daffodil. These are flowers that blossom toward the end of winter and bloom through the beginning of spring. Their appearance signals new life, new promise. The "lily" might be a lotus or a hyacinth. Its blooming period follows that of the first flowers. These are both probably merely generic references for flowers. The modifying phrases may tell us more about them than any floral identification itself.

Sharon is the fertile plain on the Mediterranean side of Palestine's central mountain range. It extends north from the seaside city of Joppa toward but not quite reaching Mount Carmel. In ancient times the combination of swampy lowlands and sandy hills made this area quite productive. The "rose of Sharon" could be any number of flowers that sprang up in this vicinity. The only other place where this bloom is mentioned in the Scriptures is in a prophetic passage describing the glories of a restored Israel (Isa 35:1). In that context it too suggests the blossoming forth of new life, new promise. In Egypt the lotus blossom is a symbol of regeneration. It too is found in a prophetic description of restoration (Hos 14:5-6 [MT 14:6-7]). All of this suggests that the new blossoming of the flowers is the tenor of both of the metaphors used to describe the woman. Just as the appearance of these flowers is a signal of life's burgeoning forth, so the woman herself represents the newness that comes with deep love and the regeneration of life that such love effects.

The man now picks up the loving exchange. By means of a well-known metaphor (lily among thorns), he redirects attention from the blossoming of the lily to its uniqueness. Everything around it is spiny or harsh, even repulsive in comparison with the woman. In like manner, his lover (*ra‘yātî*) far surpasses other maidens. The poem does not indicate in what area she surpasses them; the tenor of the metaphor is not obvious. It might be in beauty, since earlier the man praised her for this very feature (v. 15). However, as the woman used the lily metaphor, it directed our attention to its blossoming forth with new life (2:1). Since no other reference has been suggested, we can conclude that the same tenor is operative in the second instance of its appearance. In other words, the man is proclaiming that his lover is like a delicate flower that promises new life, and everything else is thorny, even life-threatening, in comparison.

The mutuality of the couple's admiration is seen in the woman's response which in form and content imitates the man's comment (vv. 2, 3a):

a   like a lily

b   among brambles

c   so my love *(ra'yātî)*

d   among maidens

a'   like an apple

b'   among trees

c'   so my love *(dôdî)*

d'   among young men

The apple as we know it today was probably not grown in ancient Israel. However, some variety of the fruit found its way into Sumerian marriage mythology. Some commentators think that, because the root of the word *(tappûaḥ)* means "to breathe, pant," it is an allusion to scent. Some of them suggest that the word would be better translated "apricot," which is a sweet-smelling tree. At issue is the tenor of the comparison, not the exact identification of the tree. Though the allusion is to some kind of fruit-bearing tree, the tree itself seems to be wild, growing in a forest or thicket, not a cultivated tree as one would expect to find in an orchard. In such a woodland, only the stalwart trees thrive. The comparisons of the lily and the tree suggest that the two lovers are not only unparalleled in their desirability, but they are also strong enough to survive in inhospitable surroundings such as their love seems to have to endure.

In describing her lover, the woman further develops the metaphor of tree, focusing on the shade that it provides and the fruit that it produces. The shade of the tree is an allusion to the man's overshadowing protection; his fruit refers to his lovemaking, particularly his passionate kisses, which she finds sweet to the taste, even better than wine (1:2). The word for "taste" *(ḥēk),* really means "mouth" or "palate," suggesting that the tasting occurs deep within the mouth and not merely in the front taste buds. The implication here is that there is full enjoyment of the fruits of love, not merely a sampling of them. The overshadowing that the man provides for his beloved is not unlike the embrace in which she held him, when as a bag of myrrh he lay upon her breasts (1:14). There is no gender stereotyping here. The passion that the couple experience and the shelter that they provide are mutual. At times she is in control; at other times he is.

The setting shifts again. This time it moves from the woodlands to some kind of enclosure (vv. 4-6). It is unlikely that what is envisioned is a public banquet hall or house of wine, for the lovers would not find there the privacy that their lovemaking seeks. It is possible that the description is meant to be understood figuratively rather than literally. It is well known that lovers will exaggerate the features of any place of trysting, for the lovemaking itself is the enjoyment that they crave, and this lovemaking can metaphorically transform any place into a garden or a royal chamber. If the man's kisses can be compared to wine, then wherever these kisses are exchanged could well be considered a banquet hall or house of wine.

The word that is often translated "intention" *(degel)* might be better rendered "banner, standard." It appears in other places as a military image, an image that would have little meaning here. However, it was not uncommon then, nor is it uncommon today, that taverns or pubs frequently would display outside of their establishments some kind of a sign, such as an overflowing flagon, indicating the pleasures that transpire inside. This may be the meaning of the reference here. The standard or intention of the man is love, and in some way he displays this, at least to his lover. However the word is understood, the meaning is clear. It is not only the woman who is in pursuit of love; the man also takes active steps in seeking opportunity for making love. Once again, the mutual character of the pursuit of love is clearly seen.

Even the thought of being led by her lover into a trysting place makes the woman faint with love. She issues a twofold request:

a   sustain me

b   with raisins

a'   refresh (support) me

b'   with apples

She is asking for food, but is this food for nourishment or are the raisins and apples really aphrodisiacs? Raisins are akin to wine, since they both come from the grape. The word for "raisins" *(ʾăšîšâ)* is translated "raisin cakes" in Hosea (3:1) where they are linked to the fertility cults. Apples too have erotic connotations. Furthermore, they are the fruit of the very tree to which the man is compared (v. 3). The verb translated "refresh" *(rappēdû)* really means "support." The woman desires the support that is provided by her lover. Overcome with love-sickness, she asks for an aphrodisiac that will heighten her passion and for the support of the man that she desires. In the following verse (v. 6) she describes the kind of support she seeks. She fantasizes about and describes the embrace of her lover. With his left hand he holds her, and with his right hand he embraces or fondles her. This is the classic position in which lovers are often portrayed. This position suggests that all of her yearning has been fulfilled. Her lover has brought her to the place of lovemaking; he takes her into his arms; and he begins to make love.

The closing refrain (2:7) is a solemn adjuration directed to the daughters of Jerusalem. Oaths of this kind are usually made in the name of some deity. Here the woman substitutes a similar-sounding phrase for the names of God:

gazelles *(ṣĕbā'ôt)*   (God of) hosts *(ṣĕbā'ôt)*

wild does *('ayᵓlôt haśśādeh)*   God almighty *('ēl šadday)*

Gazelles are well known for their beauty (*ṣĕbî* means both gazelle and beauty), agility and sexual potency; the does, on the other hand, are clearly identified as animals that are untamed and free. These are apt images for the two lovers, even though both words appear in their feminine form. This feature is employed probably in order that in Hebrew "gazelles" can correspond closely with "hosts." The exact meaning of the woman's request is unclear. On the one hand, she seems to be asking that the daughters do nothing to stimulate love before its time. However, the adjuration follows a description of the lovers in a passionate embrace, and so there is no need to warn against untimely arousal. The adjuration's disjunction with what precedes it serves to heighten the uneven movement from yearning to enjoyment to separation and then to further pursuit. This very ambiguity enables the phrase to be used in different contexts with different meanings. On the other hand it may simply function as a refrain, separating one unit of the Song of Songs from another.

AN OPPORTUNITY LOST, THEN FOUND
(2:8–3:5)

The preceding adjuration brings to a close the first major unit of the Song of Songs. The scene shifts from the passionate embrace of the lovers to the swift and graceful approach of the man, indicating a new division in the poetry. This second major unit of the Song of Songs (2:8–3:5) can also be divided into two distinct parts: the woman's account of a verbal exchange between herself and her beloved (2:8-17) and her own report of her search for and meeting with him (3:1-5). Although other people appear in this unit (the man, the sentinels of the city, and the daughters of Jerusalem), only the woman speaks. She repeats the words of her beloved; she reports the encounter in the city; she directs the concluding adjuration to the daughters of Jerusalem. This demonstrates the fact that the love affair depicted in the Song of Songs is described from the woman's point of view.

The Springtime of Love: 2:8-17

The repetition of words and refrains reveals certain clear structures in this first part. It opens with mention of mountains, the gazelle, and the stag (vv. 8-9), and it closes with the same cluster of words: gazelle, stag, mountain (v. 17). This creates an inclusion that defines a section of poetry. Verses 10 and 13 both end with the same phrase of admiration spoken by the man. This repetition forms a second inclusion. These patterns further suggest a kind of chiastic structure:

A   mountains, gazelle, stag (vv. 8-9)

B   Arise, my love (v. 10b)

C   springtime (vv. 11-13b)

B'   Arise, my love (v. 13c)

A'   gazelle, stag, mountain (v. 17)

This structure indicates that the springtime of love is the major focus of
the chiasm and the central theme of the first part of this unit. The
poems in this part contain notable repetitions of words and images,
such as voice (vv. 8, 12, 14), and blooming vines/vineyards (vv. 13, 15).
Examples of parallel construction (vv. 8, 14) are also found.

Verses 8 and 9 contain carefully balanced descriptions of two moments in the movements of the man: his approach and his actions upon
his arrival:

[8]my love *(dôdî)*, look *(hinnēh-zeh)*, he is coming,

    a   leaping

    b   upon the mountains

    a'   bounding

    b'   upon the hills

[9]my love *(dôdî)* . . ., look *(hinnēh-zeh)*, he is standing . . .

    a   gazing

    b   in through the windows

    a'   looking

    b'   in through the lattice

The Hebrew word *qôl*, with which verse 8 begins, can be translated as
the noun "voice" or as the interjection "hark!" Either translation of the
word fits the context of this segment. The man comes like a gazelle
(ṣĕbî), like a young stag *(ʾayyāl)*,[1] leaping and bounding with the grace
and agility so characteristic of those animals. The interjection "look,"
followed by a participle, indicates that the action is taking place in the
present. In her excitement at the approach of her love, the woman ex-
claims, "Pay attention! Look, here he comes! Look, here he is!"

Wall, windows, and lattices suggest some kind of an enclosure with
the woman inside and the man outside looking for her within. The
plural forms of the words for "windows" and "lattices" suggest that
the man is moving from one opening to another, eagerly seeking a
glimpse of his beloved. The intensity of his desire, exemplified by his

---

[1]The masculine forms of the words used in the adjuration link this poem with,
even as they distinguish it from, the preceding segment.

swift movements to reach her, is reflected in his eyes as he searches for her. The verbs that describe the actions of the man are all in couplets, demonstrating the intensity of his fervor: leaping and bounding (v. 8); gazing and looking (v. 9); and then the woman reports what he speaks and says (v. 10). Intent on union with his lover, he calls out, "Arise and come." The sexual excitement is clear.

His plea, which forms an inclusion (vv. 10cd, 13de) consists of a balanced construction of imperative verbs followed by epithets of endearment:

a   arise

b   my love *(raʿyātî)*

b'   my fair one *(yāpātî)*

a'   come away

The imperatives are followed by a sequence of motive clauses (vv. 11-13abc) introduced by a conjunction and a demonstrative (*kî-hinnēh*, "for now"). The passage of winter and the appearance of spring are extolled. In ancient Palestine, winter was the rainy season. This explains the parallel passage:

a   winter

b   is past

a'   rain

b'   is over and gone

With winter past, spring can begin to blossom:

blooms	appear	in the earth *(ʾereṣ)*
time of singing[2]	has come	
voice of turtledove	is heard	in our land *(ʾereṣ)*
fig tree	ripens	early figs
vines in bud	give	fragrance

---

[2] The word can also mean "pruning." Vines are usually pruned at the end of winter, before the sap rises and before the other signs of spring mentioned in this poem appear. If the verb is rendered "pruning," it corresponds to the colon that precedes it. If it is rendered "singing," it corresponds to what follows. The translation of this passage follows the NRSV with some modifications.

All of these images are somehow associated with springtime, the time when nature awakens to new life. The images appeal to sight, sound, and scent. Winter, the rainy season, is over and nature is coming alive anew. This is the time of the profusion of vibrant wildflowers that cover the earth like a multicolored carpet. It is the time of the sound of the migratory turtledove recently returned from its winter haven. It is the time when the flow of sap through the fig tree begins the ripening of its fruits. It is the time of the regeneration of vines as they bring forth blossoms and give forth fragrance. These are all harbingers of springtime. They are also all fitting images of innocent love. This is the time to "arise" from the old and "come away" to the new. The delicacy of new life and the promise that it extends, the enchantment with which spring invades the senses, both evoke and mirror the splendor of the passion of these lovers. Calling the woman into springtime is really calling her into love.

The woman continues to report the words of her beloved (vv. 14-15). Verse 14 itself consists of three paired cola. The first pair (v. 14ab) contains an example of synonymous parallelism; the second (v. 14cd) and third (v. 14ef) together comprise a chiasm. Just as the man invited his beloved into the springtime of love, now he asks that she reveal herself to him. He addresses her with a new term of endearment, "my dove." This is an apt metaphor for the woman, for both the sight and the sound of the dove bespeak tenderness. The soft lines of the bird's contour and the purity of its color suggest gentleness; the sound of its cooing has a calming effect on the spirit. In addition, as mentioned above, the dove served as a messenger of love; it was also used as a representative of the goddess of love in several ancient cultures.

Here a note of inaccessibility adds something to the metaphor. This dove is hidden:

a   in the clefts

b   of the rock

a'   in the covert

b'   of the cliff

Earlier (v. 9) the man had gone from window to window, from lattice to lattice of the enclosure that held his beloved, in the hope of catching a glimpse of her. She seems to be out of his sight here as well. It is difficult to determine whether this is a feature of coquettish flirtation on her part, or the use of separation in the Song of Songs to describe the intense longing for union that the couple experiences. However, his desire for her is quite clear. In a chiastically structured poem (v. 14), he pleads with her:

A   Let me see your countenance

B   Let me hear your voice

B'   for your voice is sweet

A'   and your countenance is lovely

The man has asked to hear the voice of his loved one. She complies with his request (vv. 15-17). The shift between second- and third-person pronouns found in these verses is another example of *enallagē*. Most likely the woman's response is addressed to her beloved, with verse 16 acting as a formula that describes the mutual attachment and belonging that the lovers share. The structure of verse 15 has been called repetitive parallelism. It consists of two bicola, each of which continues internal repetition:

> Catch us foxes, little foxes
> That ruin vineyards, vineyards in blossom

This repetition creates both alliteration and assonance, giving the verse a highly musical quality. It may even have originated in a short folk song.[3] Whatever its origin, it picks up two of the major themes of the preceding segment, vineyard and blossom.

The time of first bloom is a very vulnerable time for new growth. One of the predators against which the new season's young vines must be protected is the fox cub. In its search for insects, this vivacious little animal burrows into the ground, laying bare the roots of defenseless plants. In order to protect the young vines from the danger created by these animals, fox hunting frequently became a necessary occupational sport for vinedressers. It is possible that this particular verse was part of a song or ditty popular during the spring fox hunts.

Placed on the lips of the woman, this ditty can have various meanings. We have seen that "vineyard" can refer to the woman's own sexuality. The woman has already admitted that she has not kept careful watch over her vineyard (1:6). The foxes, which in ancient Egyptian love poetry can serve as a metaphor for womanizers,[4] might be an allusion to men who could be a threat to her blossoming sexuality. There is another way this verse can be understood. The preceding

---

[3] Bloch and Bloch, *Song of Songs*, 157.
[4] Keel, *Song of Songs*, 110.

poem employed images that exemplify the burgeoning of springtime as descriptive allusions to the promises of renewal and new birth that are engendered by love. Vineyards in new bud were part of that vernal description. In this interpretation, the foxes could be an expanded metaphor representing anything that might endanger this new growth.

The formula of mutual belonging, "My beloved is mine and I am his" (v. 16a), reiterates the attachment implied in all of the various terms of endearment used throughout the poems. He is hers ("my beloved," 1:13, 14, 16; 2:3, 8, 9, 10) and she is his ("my beloved," 1:9, 15; 2:2, 10, 13). The possessive pronouns imply reciprocal giving of oneself and acceptance of the gift of the other. Every passionate sentiment, every erotic description in the Song of Songs, flows from or exemplifies the reality represented in this simple but profound declaration—"He is mine, and I am his."

The second colon of the verse answers the question that the woman herself posed in an earlier poem: Where do you pasture? (v. 6). There the Hebrew verb had no object and for that reason lent itself to two very different translations. In that first instance, the pastoral context supported understanding the verb as transitive, yielding the translation: Where do you pasture [your flock]? The setting in this case is one of passionate union rather than one of pastoral engagement, and so the intransitive reading is preferred: He feeds among the lilies. At issue in this case is the nourishment of the man, not that of his flock. The lily is probably the lotus, a flower revered in the ancient world for its regenerative powers.[5] In an earlier poem (2:1), the man used this metaphor in reference to the woman. The sexual nuances here are obvious. Pasturing is a metaphor for lovemaking. The man finds his nourishment and pleasure in making love with the woman.

The second half of the inclusion (v. 17) closes this part. It is introduced by a temporal clause, the meaning of which is ambiguous. Is the reference to the end of the day—to the afternoon breezes that blow from the sea and the lengthening of shadows as night approaches? In this case, the woman would be asking her lover to remain with her the entire day. Or is the reference to the dawn—to the early morning wind and the disappearance of darkness? In this case she would be asking him to stay with her through the night. In either case the text describes a romantic encounter between the woman and the man, an encounter that will eventually end, causing the lovers to part. Unlike the preceding segment, here it is the woman who invites and the man who must respond. This reversal of roles demonstrates once again how the lovers are in turn assertive and responsive in their mutual relationship.

[5] Ibid., 114.

In the beginning of this piece of poetry (2:8-9), the woman described her beloved as a gazelle, a young stag leaping over the mountains in order to come to her. Here at the end, she uses the same imagery. However, there is divided opinion over the meaning of two rather significant words in the last verse. This has resulted in two very different ways of interpreting it. First, the Hebrew verb *sōb* can mean either "turn away from" or "return." The identification of the mountain (*beter*) is another point of uncertainty. Some commentators believe that it is the proper name of a specific mountain.[6] Others maintain that it is an allusion to the breasts of the woman. Still others consider it a reference to a spice-producing location. All of these differences conspire to make the verse a challenge to interpret.

If the verb is translated "turn away from," then the woman is urging her beloved to flee over the mountain with the same speed and agility with which he had come to her in the first place. His initial swiftness of approach would be evidence of his eagerness to be with her, to share the joys that the presence of the loved one engenders, while the speed of his departure could be precipitated by his need to flee before the morning light reveals his presence. If, on the other hand, the verb is translated "return," and *beter* refers either to the woman's breasts (4:5) or to spices (8:14), she could be pleading with her lover to return to her embrace "until the day breathes and the shadows flee." Either translation once again depicts the union/separation motif that plays such a prominent role in the Song of Songs.

The imagery employed in this first part is both delicate and bursting with life. Through the employment of various features of the blossoming of spring, the love that is experienced and shared by this couple is characterized as fresh, innocent, and productive as well as sensuously appealing. The animal metaphors capture various characteristics of the man and the woman. His enthusiasm is analogous to the agility of the gazelle or young stag; her beauty is compared to the gentleness of the dove. Unlike the movement described in earlier poems, here the man is in pursuit of the woman, who is characterized as a dove rather than a mare. What could appear to be contradictory descriptions are really metaphorical attempts to portray various features of these complex individuals and the passionate emotional attachment that they have for each other. The mélange of images betrays the inability of human language to describe the extraordinariness of a person that becomes accessible only to the gaze of love.

---

[6] For various interpretations see Tournay, *Word of God*, 85–97.

Whom My Soul Loves: 3:1-5

The second part of this second unit of the Song of Songs (3:1-5) can be further divided into three segments: the woman's search for her beloved (vv. 1-2), her encounter with the sentinels of the city (v. 3), and her reunion with her beloved (v. 4). The adjuration to the daughters of Jerusalem does not actually belong to the poem, but serves as the ending of the entire unit (v. 6). The difference between this part and the one preceding it is striking. The man, who was present in the earlier poems, is absent here. The peace and tranquillity evoked by the delicacy of springtime have been replaced by anxiety and bewilderment. The gentleness of the pastoral setting gives way to the harshness of the city. Resting in love ends abruptly and fervent searching takes over. This stark contrast may be the result of two very different and independent poems being placed one after the other. However, in the total context of the Song of Songs, it mirrors the emotional tension that lovers experience between the rapture of union and the desolation of separation.

The poem opens with the woman reclining on her bed. There is an element of similarity between this poem and the description of a dream that appears later (5:2-8). This similarity has led some commentators to regard the present poem as a dream or a romantic fantasy.[7] However, there is nothing in the poem itself to suggest either of these interpretations. Despite some of the uncharacteristic behavior of the woman, it sounds like an account of an actual event. The Hebrew *ballêylôt* is plural and can mean either "in the night," indicating time, or "night after night," indicating duration. The latter meaning suggests that she has yearned for him time and again, and this particular night her built-up desire is more than she can endure and so she goes out in search of him.

The key ideas in this segment are seeking and finding. The verb for "seek" *(biqqēš)* also means "require, desire, yearn for," a meaning that is very appropriate in the context of the Song of Songs. The phrase "whom my soul loves" is repeated in each verse, almost as a refrain. As explained earlier (1:7), *nepeš* (soul) really means "breath." Used here, it denotes the deep inner and life-giving force with which the woman loves her beloved, and furthermore, the force of emotion contained within this poem suggests the kind of search that causes one to breathe heavily. The structure of this poem (vv. 1-4) exhibits a repetition and a kind of circularity:

(v. 1b)   I sought him whom my soul loves;

(v. 1c)   I sought him, but found him not;

[7] See Gordis, *Song of Songs*, 84; Falk, *Song of Songs*, 179.

(v. 2a)   I will . . . go about the city . . .

(v. 2c)   "I will seek him whom my soul loves."

(v. 2d)   I sought him, but found him not;

(v. 3a)   They found me

as they went about in the city.

(v. 3b)   "Have you seen him whom my soul loves?"

(v. 4)   . . . I found him whom my soul loves.

The repetition of words and phrases emphasizes the emotion with which the woman conducts her search, emotion that developed during her nights of longing. Some form of the word "seek" appears in the first two verses which describe her search. The scope of her search is seen in the paired phrases "in the streets" and "in the squares." Ancient streets were narrow and labyrinthine. The squares, on the other hand, were open places where people tended to gather. Mention of both places denotes the comprehensiveness of her search. It is interesting to note that while it is the woman who does the seeking, it is she, not the man, who is found by the sentinels.

The woman's venture into the city is atypical in several ways. First, in patriarchal societies the city was the domain of men, not of women. Second, when women did go out in public, they did so under the scrutinizing watch of an older woman or a male guardian, but never unaccompanied. Third, such an excursion would have taken place in daylight, not at nighttime. Finally, women did not initiate conversation with men, not even with their husbands, and certainly not with men with whom they were not acquainted. Overcome with longing, this woman defies social propriety and ignores possible societal denunciation. In her single-mindedness she throws off all social restraint as she seeks the one whom her soul loves. Although the sentinels find her in the city, they seem to ignore her. At least they do not offer her any assistance in her search, nor do they in any way chastise her for her inappropriate behavior, at least not in this instance.

As spontaneously as she set out on her search, so abruptly does she end it; she finds the one whom her soul loves. The poem gives no details about his whereabouts, his activity, or where he was eventually found. There is no interest in such details. It is clear that the poem is concerned with the sentiments and movements of the woman, not with those of the man. She is the subject of the verbs in this poem; he is not. She is the one who searches and calls, who seeks and finds, who holds her love, and who brings him into the house of her mother. She finds

him in the city, presumably in a public place, and she leads him back
into a place of privacy. The parallel construction underscores a sexual
allusion:

a   house of

b   my mother

a'   house of

b'   the one who conceived me

The mother is described as the one who conceived, not as the one who
gave birth. In this instance, birth does not seem to be as important as
sexual intercourse. There is no explicit mention here of any passionate
embrace when the lovers are finally united, but the erotic intentions of
the woman are obvious. Each time there has been some kind of enclosure, it has been for the purpose of making love—the chamber into
which the man brings the woman (1:4), the room with the couch upon
which they lie in each other's arms enjoying the delights of lovemaking
(1:12), the banqueting house within which the couple prepare for making love (2:4), and now the house of the one whose sexual activity
contributed to the life of the woman. The erotic connotations are unmistakable. This last verse creates a kind of inclusion. As the poem
begins, the woman is on her bed, presumably in her room. It ends with
her bringing her lover into the house of the one who conceived her.[8]

The entire unit is brought to conclusion by an adjuration directed to
the daughters of Jerusalem (v. 5), the words of which are identical to
those that closed the first major unit of the Song of Songs (2:7). As in
that first instance, a thematic disjunction seems to appear between the
adjuration itself and the poem that precedes it. The poem paints a scene
of passionate exchange, while the adjuration asks that the daughters do
nothing to arouse love. This suggests that the adjuration functions here
as a refrain.

---

[8] Though the text does not explicitly state it, some commentators argue that this
is the very room where the woman was conceived. Such an interpretation makes the
woman's intentions even more obvious.

RAVISHED BY BEAUTY

(3:6–5:1)

The third major unit of the Song of Songs (3:6–5:1) is a mixture of various poetic forms and extravagant images. It begins with a poem describing the extraordinary character of a phenomenon that comes out of the wilderness (vv. 6-11). It is difficult to attribute this poem to any particular voice. Because the segment ends with an address to the daughters of Zion, characters who are always addressed by the woman, some assign the poem to her. Those who maintain that it is actually the woman who is coming up from the wilderness assign it to an unknown voice. This segment is unusual in the entire collection of poems, because it is a straightforward description of things rather than a metaphoric characterization of the charms of the lovers or of the passion that they share. This graphic report is followed by two poems attributed to the man: a *waṣf* which is a unique type of Arabic poem that celebrates the beauty of the human body (4:1-7); and a second poem of admiration that is similar in form and content to earlier poems of this kind (4:8-15). Finally, there is a short romantic exchange between the woman and the man (4:16–5:1).

Solomon's Procession: 3:6-11

The interpretation of this first segment has been a point of dispute for centuries. While the Hebrew in which it is written is not difficult to translate, its precise meaning cannot be determined with certainty. The ambiguity begins with the very first words of the poem. The rhetorical question with which it opens is less a query seeking an answer than it is an exclamation with dramatic intent. The literal translation of the Hebrew *mî zōʾt ʿōlâ* is "Who is that rising?" Since the participle in this phrase is feminine in form, the obvious reference is to a woman. Most commentators contend that the description that follows is an answer to this introductory question. However, since there is neither mention of nor allusion to a woman, others maintain that the reference is to the ornate litter of Solomon that is being described. This rendering leads to the translation, "What is that coming up?"

Even those who understand the passage in this latter way believe that, although there is no explicit mention of the woman, there is a presumption that she is being carried on the litter, and that she is being brought to the man in customary ancient Near Eastern wedding fashion. There are other commentators who read the introductory exclamation as just that, a freestanding introductory exclamation with no connection to the description of the litter. They argue that the litter is really a stationary bed and that no wedding procession is being described.[1] In their rendering, the exclamation simply calls attention to the luxurious couch of the king.

Regardless of which version one chooses, it is clear that something is coming out of the wilderness, and it is preceded by or causing a column of smoke. These features call to mind elements associated with the Exodus tradition. However, there is nothing else in the poem that suggests such a connection, and so these elements should probably be interpreted metaphorically rather than literally. Advance out of the wilderness is also reminiscent of merchants' caravans that traveled across the ancient world. They frequently came out of the deserts loaded with exotic goods similar to the riches of which the furniture in this description was made. The column of smoke could well refer to the fragrant clouds that emanated from burning myrrh, frankincense and other aromatic powders, also goods brought by traveling merchants.

The wilderness out of which this enigmatic phenomenon proceeds is in stark divergence from the lush vernal settings of the previous poems, although it can refer to the steppe where flocks were often pastured (1:8). Rather than considering it an actual geographic feature, we may understand the harshness that the image represents here as a point of contrast with the exorbitant luxury being described. This majestic appearance on the horizon might also call to mind the splendor of dawn rising over an eastern tract of wilderness. As it rises, it shimmers and casts a rich glow over all within its range.

The description of the furniture contains the only explicit mention of marriage in the Song of Songs (v. 11). This has led to the classification of this poem as an epithalamium, a poem in honor of a bride and groom. If this is the case, then the description could be of a wedding

---

[1] See Fox, *Song of Songs*, 120–4; Bloch and Bloch, *Song of Songs*, 160–3.

cortege that brings the bride to the bridegroom. The triple mention of Solomon (vv. 7, 9, 11) furthers the royal fiction that is often used to celebrate the wedding couple (1:4). If the various references to Solomon are merely poetic allusions, as is the position advanced here, then the entire poetic segment can be seen as a metaphoric characterization rather than a description of an actual event.

In keeping with the idea of a royal marriage cortege, the litter or portable bed is surrounded by an honor guard of sixty warriors (*gibbōrîm*), mighty men of Israel.[2] The customary size of such a guard was thirty men.[3] The double size of the entourage marks the extraordinary importance of this procession. Its military character serves a twofold purpose; one is practical and the other is dramatic. First, it guarantees protection from any and all threats that the procession might encounter. Second, the very power that it exhibits adds to the solemnity and grandeur of the procession itself. The swords of the warriors are sheathed, not drawn, as would be the case in a situation of imminent military threat. By the very nature of his position, a king would have to be protected. However, the dangers that are mentioned here are the "terrors of the night" (see Ps 91:5). Perhaps this is a reference to those demons who were thought to threaten the conjugal bed (see Tob 6:14-15).

The identification of the second piece of furniture, the palanquin, is even more difficult to determine. It is believed to be a sedan chair or some kind of canopied construction. The unusual Hebrew word is probably of Persian or Greek origin, and it appears in no other place in the Bible. Some consider it merely a synonym for litter and believe that the entire segment is a description of one and the same piece of transportable furniture.[4] There is difficulty in this interpretation, for the text says that Solomon made the carriage for himself, while it is inferred that the litter is for carrying the woman. While the descriptions are probably of two different pieces of furniture, there are certain structural parallels between them. First, both the litter and the carriage are explicitly identified as belonging to Solomon. Second, there are six cola describing the military guard of the litter and six cola describing the magnificence of the canopied carriage. Some commentators believe that the latter is a stationary canopied throne similar to the kind before which Israelite kings were believed to have been married.[5] Still others

---

[2] This is the only time the name Israel appears in the Song of Songs.

[3] As found in the wedding ceremony of Samson (Judg 14:11) and the retinue of David (2 Sam 23:18-19, 23).

[4] Elliott, *Literary Unity*, 86.

[5] Goulder, *Song of Fourteen Songs*, 29.

maintain that it is not a piece of furniture at all but a pavilion that housed the royal litter.[6]

Many of the words in the description of the palanquin are found in no other place in the Bible, leaving numerous questions about the palanquin's actual construction. Whether this is a portable or a stationary object, it is clear that it is constructed of and decorated with the most exquisite and luxurious materials—cedar, silver, gold, purple cloth. The wood from Lebanon was renowned throughout the ancient Near Eastern world for its excellent quality. The silver posts could be either the poles used for carrying the sedan chair, the supports of the canopy, or the pillars that formed the base of the stationary throne. The gold back could be couch coverings upon which one could recline, or an elaborate overhead canopy. Purple coloring, traditionally identified as a royal color, most likely came from the murex shellfish, a sea creature that was found in abundance on the Mediterranean coast and whose shades ranged from red to violet or blue-black. Cushions of this color upon which to sit or recline were a sign of royalty or opulence.

The final colon of this description of the palanquin is the most obscure of all. The Hebrew *ʾahăbâ*, ordinarily translated as "love," can also mean "leather."[7] The latter translation is probably the better choice in this case. However, the passionate character of the Song of Songs suggests that the first meaning is also very appropriate. Actually, both meanings might apply here. The reference may be to an elaborate leather interior, which was artistically decorated with romantic art. Such a feature could be part of either portable or stationary furniture.

Whether these descriptions point to the presence of one or two pieces of furniture, and whether that furniture is portable or stationary, the extraordinariness portrayed is undeniable. Although they are not concerned with any of the human emotions that flow from or result in passionate love, the elegance that they depict acts as a context within which these emotions can find a home. They exemplify the expression "Nothing is too good for the one I love!" If the entire passage was originally a description of a wedding procession, it only adds a note of grandeur to the celebration of the couple's unabashed passion. If it originated as the depiction of a cavalcade of a king, it contributes to the royal fiction that is used to characterize the couple. In either case, the description of this breathtaking spectacle leaves no doubt about the majesty of the love itself.

The segment ends with an address structured in three bicola. It contains imperatives directed to the daughters of Zion. The first and third

[6] Fox, *Song of Songs*, 126–7.
[7] Elliott, *Literary Unity*, 302, n. 97.

bicola are in synonymous parallel construction; the middle one contains a repetition of the word "crown." This kind of chiastic pattern, determined by parallel structure rather than content, highlights the middle bicolon, which states that the king was crowned by his mother. The literary unity of this address is confirmed by artistic use of alliteration and assonance; each bicola begins with the sound of "b" and ends with the sound of "ô."

A   a   daughters *(bĕnôt)* of Jerusalem

       b   come out

       b'   look

       a'   daughters *(bĕnôt)* of Zion *(ṣîyôn)*

B   at King *(bammelek)* Solomon *(šĕlōmōh),*

            at the crown *(bāʿăṭārâ)* with which his mother crowned him *(lô ʾimmô)*

A'   a   on the day *(bĕyôm)*

       b   of his wedding *(ḥătunnātô)*

       a'   on the day *(bĕyôm)*

       b'   of the gladness of his heart *(libbô).*

The text clearly states that the crown was placed on the king's head on the day of his marriage, indicating that this was probably a wedding wreath rather than a royal crown. Once again we find the involvement of a mother, but not that of a father. This seems to have been a common feature of ancient Egyptian love poems.[8] Here it might also correspond to a detail in the biblical story of Solomon, where we read that his mother was very influential in securing for him succession to the throne of his father David (see 1 Kgs 1:11-31). In a sense, she did indeed place the crown on his head. Here that detail fits both the scene of a wedding procession and the royal fiction that is so prominent in the Song of Songs.

As already stated, this poem seems to be out of place in the Song of Songs. It describes neither the lovers nor the places where they meet to experience their mutual passion. However, it does contain features that link it with the other poems. There is mention of the myrrh and frankincense (v. 8; 1:13; 4:6, 14). The smoke and fragrance that they produce could well generate a fantasy of such splendor. The litter/palanquin

---

[8] Keel, *Song of Songs*, 136–7.

calls to mind the couch of the king (v. 12). It would, in all probability, serve as the bed for making love. In the eyes of lovers, any such bed would be envisioned as being made of priceless materials and surrounded with intoxicating aromas. Finally, the honor guard, which serves to heighten the importance of the bed, links this poem to the description of the woman that follows (4:4d). The poem may have had an origin that was very different from the other love poems, but it has been artistically woven into the fabric of the Song of Songs.

An Ode to Her Body: 4:1-7

This poem contains several interesting literary characteristics. First, it begins and ends with an exclamation of the beauty of the woman, thus forming an inclusion (vv. 1, 7):

(v. 1) you are beautiful, my love *(raʿyātî)*

(v. 7) you are beautiful, my love *(raʿyātî)*

Second, the opening element of the inclusion is an exact repetition of a phrase found in an earlier poem (1:15). Third, with one exception the poem is composed of a series of nominal clauses that function paratactically (without the use of conjunctive words) as comparisons. Fourth and perhaps most significantly, the poem itself is an example of a *waṣf*, an Arabic poem that describes part by part the body of the beloved. It is a descriptive song that uses metaphors or similes both representationally (highlighting physical similarity) and presentationally (eliciting an emotional response).

Although there is no strict literary pattern to which the entire poem conforms, there are some definite structural characteristics besides the initial inclusion. It begins with three bicola (vv. 1b-2b), all of which follow the same word order. The physical feature of the woman is mentioned first; this feature is compared to something from the animal world; there is then an elaboration of the feature:

your eyes	doves	behind your veil
your hair	flocks of goats	moving down the slopes
your teeth	flocks of ewes	coming up from washing

The series closes with a final bicolon (v. 2cd) which further develops the last element within it:

all of which bear twins	none among them is bereaved

A set of three similes follows (vv. 3-4b). The syntactic pattern of this group differs from the first. Here the vehicle of the comparison precedes mention of the physical feature; elaboration of the feature completes the phrase:

like crimson thread	your lips	your mouth is lovely
like pomegranate halves	your cheeks	behind your veil
like tower of David	your neck	built in courses

This second series closes in the same way as the first series closed, with a bicolon that further develops the last element within it:

a thousand bucklers hang on it   all of them shields of warriors

The final comparison of the *waṣf* (v. 5) is a tricolon that follows the syntactic order of the first series. The physical feature is mentioned; a comparison is made; an elaboration completes the phrase:

your breasts   fawns/twins of gazelle   that feed among the lilies

There are striking similarities between verses 5b-6 and 2:16b-17. However, the subjects are reversed. In the earlier passage (2:16b) the man was likened to a gazelle that fed among the lilies, here (4:5b) the comparison is to the breasts of the woman. 2:17 and 4:6 are also similar, the first bicolon of each containing exactly the same wording. The differences are found in the second bicolon and in the fact that the man was addressed in the earlier poem, while here he speaks and states his resolve.

The *waṣf* is an example of the Ancient Near Eastern custom of portraying favored features of a person in the guise of the strength or beauty of the surrounding world. Some of the imagery may seem strange, even crude, to modern thinking. However, a careful examination of the metaphor will reveal the appropriateness of the tenor despite the apparent awkwardness of the vehicle. The admiration expressed in the verses that constitute the inclusion (vv. 1ab, 7a) shows that the metaphors were prized both for their representational and their presentational value. We must remember that poetry often loses the strength of its impact if it is read in a purely literal fashion. Furthermore, read in that way, it might even appear to contradict some of the images it has already portrayed. For example, this *waṣf* extols the beauty of the woman's eyes, her hair, her teeth, her lips, her cheeks, her neck, and her breasts. Yet twice it states that she is veiled. While a diaphanous veil could still reveal the contours of these features, it would attenuate the sharpness of the colors that seem to be evident to the eye. The *waṣf*, like all poetry, must be read imagistically if it is to be appreciated.

The woman's eyes have already been compared to doves (1:15). However, here they are said to be behind a veil. The exact nature of the veil is difficult to determine.[9] It does not seem to be a yashmak, the kind of covering worn by some Near Eastern women that has only eye-slits and which conceals the identity of the wearer (see Gen 24:65; 38:14, 19). In fact her dark complexion, which was commented on in an earlier poem (1:5) leads one to conclude that she was not normally veiled. The marriage motif in the previous poem suggests that this could be a wedding veil, but there is nothing in the present context to support this. The veil itself is certainly intended for some degree of conceal-ment. However, it seems to be the kind of concealment that beguiles rather than hides. It could be the kind of face veil that covers most of the face but which actually emphasizes the eyes. Such a veil accentu-ates the mysteriousness of the woman's eyes and makes them even more alluring. This veil seems to act as a tease. Both the representa-tional and the presentational interpretations are obvious.

The woman's hair is compared to goats streaming down the slopes of Gilead, a district in Transjordan that was noted for its rugged cliffs. The tenor of this metaphor is rich in meaning and dynamic in details. The comparison could be based on color, the apparent undulating movement of the flock, the length of the vision that they create, or the vitality of their gait. Actually, all of these characteristics can be applied to the woman's hair. For the most part, goats in Syria-Palestine were coal black. The metaphor suggests the same color for the woman's hair. The primary feature of the image seems to be the movement of the flock. It courses down the mountainside like a flowing stream, moving up and down as rippling water does. This movement suggests both the cascading movement of her hair down her head, neck and shoulders and the waviness of the hair itself. A large flock suggests long, flowing hair. This dynamic image is reinforced by the spirited character of goats. Unlike sheep that can be easily led, goats have been traditionally regarded as frolicsome, even unrestrained. So is the woman's rippling hair.

Although the metaphor is applied to her hair and not to the woman herself, hair has been associated with various human traits. Besides being a symbol of power (Samson) it can also imply unruliness (see Ps 68:21 [MT 68:22]; Dan 4:33). Even today, disheveled hair suggests that one is somehow unfettered by social protocol. Here the metaphor cap-tures a sense of the loveliness of the woman's hair (representational),

---

[9] "Locks," "tresses," or "braided hair" rather than "veil" have been advanced as alternative translations of the Hebrew word ṣammâ; see Bloch and Bloch, *Song of Songs*, 166–8.

and its free-flowing buoyancy creates a sense of excitement (presentational).

The man's attentive and loving gaze has moved from the woman's fascinating eyes down to her luxurious flowing hair, and now to her teeth. The image of a flock of black goats used above is balanced here with that of a flock of white sheep. The first flock was described as moving down the mountains in an energetic flow; this flock is said to have come up out of the water, having been washed in preparation for shearing. Although there is movement in this picture as well, the metaphor is more interested in the color of the ewes and their offspring and in their orderly arrangement in pairs. The fact that they have been washed implies that their wool is now clean, even white. By implication, so are the teeth of the woman.

The ewes are said to have produced twins, sets of offspring. Furthermore, not one ewe in the flock is bereaved. In other words, the sets are intact. Again by implication, so are the teeth of the woman. The upper teeth correspond to the lower teeth. Scholars contend that twin births in sheep were very unusual in the ancient world. The poet may be making the point that as unlikely as were twin births, so unusual was a full set of teeth. The image portrayed is of sheep, white from having been washed, standing paired and in rows waiting to be sheared. The fact that the man knows so well what his beloved's teeth look like indicates that he has seen her smile, a sign of either familiarity or coquetry. This metaphor not only describes another feature of the woman's appearance (representational) but it also seeks to underscore the extraordinariness of this particular feature in order to elicit a sense of admiration (presentational).

The man continues to extol the beauty of his beloved's mouth, turning his attention to her lips.[10] The Hebrew word *midbār* can be translated as "speech" or as "lips," organs of speech. Both the character of the *waṣf* itself, the vehicle of the metaphor (crimson thread), and the addition of the homonym (mouth) clearly indicate that the primary reference here is to her lips, though the secondary meaning (speech) opens the metaphor to another level of interpretation.[11] He compares her lips to a scarlet thread. The tenor could be to the color, or the thread-thinness, or both. Red is the color that is often associated with love or sex (see Josh 2:18; Jer 4:30). There is evidence that Egyptian women painted their lips in order to enhance their attractiveness, and it is likely that women of other ancient Near Eastern societies did so as

[10] Although the next three comparisons are really similes containing the comparative term *kě* ("like"), they will be referred to as metaphors in the analysis.

[11] Fox, *Song of Songs*, 129–30.

well. The thinness of the cord may have nothing to do with this metaphor, or it could suggest that the woman is smiling, as suggested above in the explanation of her teeth, in which case her lips would be narrower than usual. In a smile, brilliant red lips would accentuate the whiteness of her teeth and vice versa.

The descriptive phrase that further develops this comparison is unusual. It is the only adjectival clause in the series of descriptive nominal clauses. Thus far the poet has used vivid visual imagery in the comparisons. Here a simple descriptive phrase with a single adjective is used, and the description itself is quite vague ("your mouth is lovely"). It might be that a concrete visual noun is not used because of the double meaning of *midbār*. Once again the metaphor functions in both a representational and a presentational manner. The tenor addresses both the brilliant color and the thin shape of the woman's mouth, and it also suggests that her mouth is partially open in a smile, an expression that can be quite titillating. Finally and most importantly, her brilliantly colored mouth is an invitation to the deep and passionate kissing that she herself has already alluded to in the very first poem (1:2).

The vehicle of the next metaphor, the sliced pomegranate, is compared to yet another of the woman's facial features. There is some question about the meaning of the Hebrew word *raqqâ*. It can be translated "temple" (see Judg 4:21, 22; 5:26) or even "brow." The most common rendering has been "cheek." However, the reference is not to the entire pomegranate, but to a slice of it. This detail makes it difficult to determine exactly what tenor was intended. If attention is given to the outer part of the fruit, its blush-red skin and its rounded contour might be a reference to rosy cheeks. On the other hand, a slice of the fruit would reveal its inner fleshy red membranes and white seeds, suggesting the interior of the woman's mouth. This interpretation would correspond to the previous descriptions of her mouth and teeth.

The pomegranate itself was esteemed both for its sweet taste and its symbolic value. Though it is used here in reference to a facial feature, the sensual connotations that it carries would not have gone unnoticed. Its color, its contour, and its softness are themselves quite provocative. Its plump shape and its profusion of seeds made it a fitting symbol of fertility, and for this reason it was used extensively in ancient Near Eastern art.[12] Furthermore, the fruit and the juice that was extracted from it were widely regarded as aphrodisiacs. Although the exact reference here is unclear, the sexual nuances associated with this fruit influence whichever way it is understood. As has been the case with each comparison in this *waṣf*, this vividly graphic and emotionally tantaliz-

[12] Keel, *Song of Songs*, 143–7.

ing metaphor functions in both a representational and a presentational fashion. It describes the facial feature and it calls to mind erotic enjoyment. The metaphor concludes with the descriptive phrase "behind your veil." The phrase forms a kind of inclusion, which brackets the man's praise of the woman's facial beauty: (v. 1) "eyes . . . behind your veil"; (v. 3) "cheeks . . . behind your veil." Here again, the veil actually augments her mysteriousness and serves to enhance her attractiveness, her inaccessibility, and her consequent desirability.

Having completed his praise of his beloved's head and face, the man turns his attention to her neck, comparing it to the tower of David. Such a comparison may sound uncomplimentary to contemporary Western sensitivities, but the vehicle of the metaphor carries some very impressive connotations. It is not clear to which tower the man refers. He may have no particular tower in mind. The name David *(dāwîd)* may have been chosen simply because it is very close in sound to the principal term of endearment which the woman uses for the man *(dôdî,* my love).[13] An interpretation of this play on sounds sets up a very interesting expression of mutual possession; he is her love, while she is his tower.

Although towers are often considered phallic symbols, here the vehicle clearly carries a different meaning. The reference might be to the tower's grace and stateliness. Even today long, arching necks are considered quite beautiful. Ancient towers were usually massive, and so the metaphor might suggest power and determination. Actually, the phrase that elaborates the comparison suggests that the primary focus of the simile is not the tower itself, but something about its appearance; it is "built in courses" *(talpîyôt)*. This Hebrew word is found in no other place in the Bible, and so from the beginning it has yielded various interpretations.[14] However, it is generally understood to mean that the tower was constructed in regular rows of squared stones.

Warriors frequently hung their shields on the battlements of such towers. This would explain the bucklers and shields mentioned in the poem. The custom gave the tower an appearance of ornate splendor. Although the image is one of martial grandeur, the metaphor itself seems to be less interested in the military character of the tower than its adornments. The embellishment of the tower is probably the tenor of this metaphor. Just as in an earlier poem, the woman was compared to one of the mares in the stables of Pharaoh, a mare adorned with elaborate ornaments and strings of jewels (1:9), so here her ornamented neck

[13] See Exum, "Literary and Structural Analysis," 62.

[14] Pope, *Song of Songs,* 465–8. For an entirely different interpretation see Bloch and Bloch, *Song of Songs,* 170–3.

is likened to a tower embellished with elaborate military trappings. The rows of bucklers and shields imply that she is wearing strand upon strand of jewelry, a custom that was quite common in the ancient world. This is the only metaphor in the *waṣf* that does not extol an actual physical feature of the woman. Instead, it marvels at the splendor with which she adorns her body. The tenor of the metaphor clearly links, in a representational manner, the decorations hung on the tower with necklaces worn by the woman. The sentiment that it presentationally elicits is admiration.

The poem moves from the severe military image to a scene of gentle pastoral enjoyment. The breasts of the woman are compared to two gazelle fawns. We have already seen that gazelles are known for their grace and beauty. In ancient Near Eastern art they are often associated with love goddesses and are found in depictions of the tree of life.[15] This is clear evidence of their importance as symbols of fertility. The fawns of the gazelle suggest not only tawny coloring and the touch of softness, but youth and firmness, even playfulness. The sexual implications of the comparison are augmented by mention of the lilies, lotus flowers that are also symbols of regeneration (see 2:1-2). This metaphor shows that the imagery used here is gender-neutral, for in an earlier poem it was the man who was compared to a gazelle that feeds among the lilies (see 2:16).

An obvious similarity, yet with distinct difference, exists between verses 6 and 2:17 as well. There we find an allusion to the time of day and a reference to mountains. Actually, the first lines of each verse are identical. It is in the further descriptions of the mountains that the passages differ, as well as in the fact that in the earlier poem the woman speaks to the man and here the man speaks to her. Despite these minor differences, the significant similarities suggest that many of the sensual allusions and erotic sentiments that are so prominent in the first passage, are by association carried over into the second passage. As with the earlier poem, it is not clear whether the time reference is to the end of the day with the lengthening of shadows or to dawn with the disappearance of darkness. Regardless of which time of day is intended, it is a moment for mutual enjoyment of each other.

The fascination with the woman's breasts just described in the *waṣf*, and the earlier association of her breasts with a sachet of myrrh (see 1:13), may explain the mention of mountains in this passage. "Mountain of myrrh" and "hill of frankincense" should be considered an example of parallel construction rather than a reference to two different elevations. Furthermore, since neither of these aromatic resins is indi-

---

[15] Keel, *Song of Songs*, 91.

genous to Israel, the reference is probably not to any geographic location but is a poetic allusion. The referent of the metaphor is certainly the overpowering charms of the woman. Though not explicitly stated here, given the surrounding imagery and the associations with earlier poems, it is difficult not to imagine the man hastening to her breasts in anticipation of a passionate embrace.

A second declaration of the woman's beauty (v. 7) completes the inclusion and brings the *waṣf* to its conclusion, even though it describes only the upper portion of the woman's body. The man's declaration supplements his praise of her beauty in two ways. He adds a qualifying term *(kullāk)* which means "the whole of you, every inch of you." This implies that it was not necessary to extol every part of her body to know that it was "altogether beautiful." He ends by declaring that she is without flaw. The Hebrew word translated "flaw" *(mûm)* generally refers to physical defect. The phrase is usually used to describe the perfect condition of the animals that are offered in sacrifice. As strange as this reference may sound to contemporary people, it suggests the greatest compliment that can be applied to the woman's physical appearance. Not only does she please the man who loves her, but her body is recognized as perfect in every way.

Throughout the *waṣf* the man uses various metaphors that extol his beloved's physical beauty, which is sexually attractive to him. He uses imagery from both pastoral and urban settings (the slopes of Gilead, the tower of David), and he compares her to animals that are both domesticated (goats and sheep) and undomesticated (doves and gazelles). Mention of his hastening to the mountains suggests his desire for union with her, not the realization of it. This song of admiration ends with an expression of deep yearning, a trait so characteristic of the Song of Songs.

My Garden, My Bride: 4:8–5:1

Although this third part of the third unit of the Song of Songs enjoys unity within itself, it can still be divided into three discernible segments with an introductory invitation: the invitation (v. 8), a general description of delight in the beauty of the woman (vv. 9-11), characterization of the woman as a garden (vv. 12-15), an exchange between the woman and the man (4:16–5:1). This division and the other major literary techniques found here are determined by vocabulary. For example, there are three references to Lebanon (vv. 8, 11, 15); two of them form an inclusion which sets the limits of the first segment, and the third brings the second segment to conclusion. This is the only place in the

Song of Songs where the Hebrew word for bride *(kallâ)* is found, and it appears six times in only nine verses. Other literary techniques include a chiastic pattern formed by the use of *kallâ* as well as the internal repetition of other words (vv. 8-11). This part contains examples of paronomasia or play on the words *lĕbānôn* (Lebanon)/*lĕbônâ* (frankincense) and *bāśām* (spice)/*śemen* (oil). Finally, this part contains the only example in the Song of Songs of a sustained metaphor (4:12–5:1).

Verse 8 seems to be an interruption in the man's praise of the beauty of his beloved. It belongs neither to the preceding *waṣf* nor to the following song of admiration. Though quite brief, it can be considered a poem of yearning. Placed here, it is connected to the preceding *waṣf* by the reference to mountains and the catchword "frankincense" (v. 6). It is connected to what follows by its mention of "bride," a name used here as a term of endearment and not as an identification of marital status. This single verse itself is well crafted with several examples of internal parallelism:

> with me from Lebanon, bride,
>
> with me from Lebanon
>
> > come
>
> > depart	from peak of Amana
>
> > > from peak of Senir and Hermon
>
> > > from dens of lions
>
> > > from mountains of leopards

The verbs "come" and "depart" are imperfect in form, suggesting more a wish than an invitation, which would be expressed with an imperative form of the verb. The image created here is reminiscent of an episode in Canaanite mythology, where the shepherd Tammuz/Adonis flees with his beloved to the mountains of Lebanon.[16] Amana, Hermon and Senir (the Amorite name for Hermon) are all peaks in the Anti-Lebanon range of the Lebanon Mountains. These majestic summits were known not only for their pristine beauty but also because they appeared to be inaccessible. In ancient times they constituted a forested range infested with lions and leopards, making the mountains even more unapproachable. There might be a second trace of mythology here, for lions and leopards were often pictured with the Assyrian goddess Ishtar.[17]

---

[16] Pope, *Song of Songs*, 475-7.
[17] Keel, *Song of Songs*, 158-60.

The man is not asking that the woman go away with him *to* Lebanon, but that she come *from* Lebanon. There is a note of ambiguity here. The opening word of the verse has been understood in two different ways: *ʾittî* (with me), or by emendation as *ʾĕtî* (come). The first rendering would suggest that both the woman and the man are in Lebanon and he is inviting her to return from Lebanon *with* him. The second rendering would have her returning *to* him. Most likely these references are not to actual geography, but are intended as figurative allusions to the general unapproachableness of the woman. This theme has already appeared in an earlier poem, where the woman was said to be hidden away in the clefts of the rock/the recesses in the cliff, another high and inaccessible place (2:14). Both versions acknowledge the woman's inaccessibility. Even if the man is with her, it can still mean that no one else was able to approach her.

The invitation or wish is followed by a song of admiration (vv. 9-11). Each verse is composed of tricola. In them are found various poetic techniques—forms of parallel construction, repetition of words, paronomasia, alliteration, onomatopoeia. The metaphors used in these three verses all appeal to sensual delights of sight (v. 9), taste (vv. 10-11b), or smell (v. 11c).

The parallel construction of verses 9 and 10 is striking:[18]

[9]you ravished my heart		my sister-bride
you ravished my heart	with a glance	of your eyes
	with a jewel	of your necklace(s)
[10]how beautiful your love		my sister-bride
how better	your love	than wine
	the fragrance of your oils	than spice

The verb translated "ravish" is denominative, derived from the noun *lēb* (heart). There are very few instances in the Bible where the heart is meant simply as a physical organ. Instead, it is usually used metaphorically to refer to various aspects of the human personality, such as the discerning mind, the memory, the desires and the will. The ancients did not consider these functions as emotionless. Rather, all of these functions were infused with some degree of emotion. Any verb derived from this noun would carry this same rich and multifaceted meaning. The form of the verb used here can be understood as causative (intensifying an action) or as privative (depleting one). "Ravish" is a good

---

[18] Translation based on NRSV, modified by the author.

translation, since it means "to fill with strong emotion" as well as "to carry off by force." The colloquial phrase "you drive me crazy" also captures both meanings of the verb. The man is ravished by her just as she is faint with love of him (compare 2:5; 5:8). The mutuality of their obsession with each other is plainly seen.

The favored term of endearment, "bride," is joined here by a second title, "sister." It is another pet name that is frequently found in love poetry.[19] Both "bride" and "sister" carry the meaning of physical intimacy. Although many cultures practiced some form of brother-sister marriage, sibling relatedness is also understood figuratively. When this is the case, it connotes physical bondedness, not of kinship but of passionate love. That is probably how the term should be understood here.

The man is so thoroughly under the spell of the woman that even the smallest thing can ravish his heart—a mere glance, or a single item of jewelry. The woman's eyes have already been compared to gentle, peaceful, love-inspiring doves (1:15; 4:1). Now they are said to exercise a kind of mesmerizing power over him, and they can accomplish this feat by means of a single glance. A literal reading of this verse might suggest that the man is also captivated by a single jewel in the many-stranded necklace worn by the woman. The jewelry is intended to enhance the beauty of the woman, not to capture the man's attention and to distract him from concentrating on her. The parallel construction suggests, instead, that the jewel is like an amulet, perhaps an agate eye-stone that was believed to have mystical powers. Both her eyes and this gem cast a hypnotic spell over him.

Earlier the man extolled the beauty of the woman (1:15); here, in words that repeat her praise of him (1:2a) he proclaims that her love-making is better than wine (4:10). As in the first instance, the comparison clearly suggests that the tenor of the metaphor is the intoxicating effect that wine produces. Furthermore, the plural form of the noun (*dôdîm*) implies lovemaking, as was the case in the earlier poem. The mutuality of their intoxicating love is clearly seen. First the woman declared that his lovemaking was better than wine; now her lover returns the compliment.

A second correspondence with the opening lines of the Song of Songs is found in the third colon of this verse. Initially the woman celebrated the fragrance of the man's anointing oils, the perfume of his name/person (1:3). Now, employing the paronomasia oil (*šemen*)/ spice (*bāśām*), he maintains that her anointing oils surpass the most fragrant spices. It should be remembered that the natural scents of a person combine with the perfumes with which one anoints his or her

---

[19] Fox, *Song of Songs*, xii–xiii.

body. Therefore, the aroma that is given off is frequently quite distinctive. Furthermore, this aroma is augmented by the heat and the endorphins that the body generates during lovemaking. As he was entranced by the power of her eyes, so now he is captivated by the fragrance of her person.

Verse 11 is not constructed in a parallel fashion, but it does contain an alliteration that creates an onomatopoeia. The exact meaning of the metaphor is difficult to determine. The vehicle is clearly the juice of the honeycomb and the tenor is its delectability. However, the woman's lips could refer to her kisses or to her speech. While either understanding would fit the context, the previous comparison of her lovemaking to wine suggests that kisses are the primary meaning. The fact that a metaphor can be understood in more ways than one is evidence of the artistic excellence of the poem. A further example of this artistry is the onomatopoeic alliteration. The flood of the sounds of "p" and "t" in the first colon of the verse replicates the sound of honey dripping from the honeycomb. "Milk and honey" is a familiar phrase which normally signifies fruitfulness. Here the order of the terms is reversed so that the word for "honey," with which the colon begins, corresponds to "nectar," which began the first colon:[20]

| nectar | drips from your lips |
| honey and milk | under your tongue |

The first word for honey denotes the sticky fluid produced by bees from the nectar collected from flowers; the second is the kind of honey that is produced from date-syrup, grape-syrup, or is harvested from the comb of the bee. Savory morsels are often kept under one's tongue, there to prolong the delight of taste. This reference can also be a reference to the titillating sensation engendered by tongue-kissing.

The metaphor in the final colon of the verse yields two similar yet different meanings. The scent of the woman's clothing is compared to the scent of Lebanon. This could be an allusion to the luxurious aromas that are associated with that country or, in a paronomastic manner, it could be a reference to the intoxicating bouquet of frankincense *(lĕbônâ)*. Since both interpretations describe the fragrance of the woman's clothing, and since the paronomastic connection between Lebanon and frankincense has already been made, it does not seem necessary to choose one meaning to the exclusion of the other. For the reasons already given, either interpretation would quite easily call to mind the other one. The clothing referred to is the outer garment that was used

---

[20] Translation based on NRSV, modified by author.

as a cloak during the day and as a cover for sleeping at night (compare Deut 24:13). This sensuous description (vv. 9-11), which appeals to sight and taste and scent, concludes with a veiled allusion to the woman's bed, the place where lovemaking can finally be realized.

The man's admiration of the woman continues with the only sustained metaphor in the entire Song of Songs. In it the woman is described as a garden (4:12–5:1). Two major images control the metaphors in this next segment (vv. 12-15). They are the enclosed nature of the garden and the fountain that serves as the source of its water. There is question about the wording of the second colon of the verse. The Hebrew has *gal*, which means "heap" and is here rendered by some as "pool." This reading would yield the following parallel construction:

(v. 12a)   a garden locked   my sister-bride

(v. 12b)   a pool locked

                                a fountain sealed

When the word is amended to read *gan* ("garden") it yields:

(v. 12a)   a garden locked   my sister/bride

(v. 12b)   a garden locked   a fountain sealed

The verbs seem to confirm the second reading. "Enclosed" or "locked" denotes being secured from within the enclosure; "sealed" means having some kind of fastening affixed outside of the enclosure. A garden can be locked, but it is impossible to lock a pool or spring.

However the verse is read, the meaning is fundamentally the same: the woman is not accessible to anyone but the man, who calls her by the intimate terms of endearment, "my sister-bride." The riches of the garden are delineated in verses 13 and 14, and the fountain is described in verse 15. This segment is set off as distinct not only by the explicit garden metaphor, but also by its linguistic character. Verses 12-15 contain no verbs at all, only participles that describe static conditions rather than dynamic actions. They appear to be a kind of inventory of garden plants, not unlike the onomastica discovered in ancient Egyptian documents. While the garden metaphor sets this segment off as distinct, the appellation "sister-bride" and the sensual metaphors of taste and smell link the passage with what precedes it and with what follows.

Both ancient art and literature reveal how important gardens were in the ancient world. They provided not only relaxation and pleasure but also fruits and herbs for sustenance. It is no surprise that a garden played prominently in love poetry both as a place of rendezvous and as a metaphor of female sexuality. A garden without some source of water would be unthinkable; a garden with its own source of water would be a boon. The garden described in this metaphor belongs to the latter category. It is probably the extraordinary fruitfulness of this garden with its fountain of abundant water that prompts its being enclosed, locked up, sealed against intrusion and plunder. Only those with right of access would be admitted. It is not clear from these verses whether or not the man had such a right. However, it is made clear in the next verses (4:16; 5:1).

The meaning of the word that opens the descriptive inventory, derived from the verb meaning "to send," is difficult to determine. Although it is usually translated "shoots" or "branches," some believe that it is a reference to female genitalia.[21] Whatever it actually means, by itself it does advance the garden metaphor. This is made explicit by means of the Persian loan-word *pardēs*, which is translated "park" or "orchard,"[22] and is the origin of the word "paradise." This particular word and the character of the plants that grow within the garden mark it as extraordinary, perhaps even a fantasy garden with exotic plants:

pomegranates	with choicest fruits
henna	with nard
nard and saffron, calamus and cinnamon	with frankincense
myrrh and aloes	with chief spices

The erotic significance of the pomegranate as an aphrodisiac has already been discussed (4:3). Its profusion of seeds has garnered for it the reputation of being fruitful and enjoying life-giving powers. The other plants in the garden are known for their aromatic properties.

There seems to be little if any consistency in the way these plants are listed. Sometimes the tree or plant is identified; at other times mention is made of the product that it produces and that is then distilled. Included in the garden are the fragrant henna bushes with the nard plant, the aromatic nard and saffron, the sweet-smelling cane and cinnamon, the intoxicating frankincense, and the heady myrrh and aloes.[23] Most of these spices were not indigenous to the land, but had to be imported from India, Egypt, southern Arabia, eastern Africa, or central Asia. This only added to their exotic mystique. The rarity of the

---

[21] See Pope, *Song of Songs*, 490; Fox, *Song of Songs*, 137–8; Keel, *Song of Songs*, 174–8.

[22] It is a royal orchard or forest in Neh 2:8 and Eccl 2:5.

[23] Keel describes these spices in greater detail, *Song of Songs*, 178–80.

vegetation produced by this fantastic garden suggests the exceptional nature of the woman's beauty. She is an incomparable garden, graced with beauty that is rare and unmatched.

Verse 15 turns our attention away from the exotic products of the garden to the fountain within it. From the point of view of structure, it presents a difficulty. It does not follow the pattern of the inventory of spices, and it seems forced to consider it one of the shoots or branches referred to earlier (v. 13). It may be a continuation of the introductory thought of verse 12:

(v. 12a)	a garden locked		my sister/bride
(v. 12b)	a garden locked	a fountain sealed	
....			
(v. 15)		a fountain	of gardens
		a well	of living waters
		streams	from Lebanon

In contrast to static water that has been collected in a well or cistern, this is living water, dynamic, bubbling, fresh and rejuvenating. The free flow of this water seems to contradict the notion of a sealed fountain, unless we remember that the poem is dealing with metaphors of a fantasy paradise, not a precise description of a real garden. In the first reference to the fountain, its inaccessibility is the tenor of the metaphor; here its life-giving quality is the point of comparison. Like streams flowing down the slopes of the Lebanon range, this water is continuously replenished and renewed, an apt image of the life-giving potential of the woman. Both the garden and the fountain possess unbelievable magnificence and fecundity, fitting metaphors for portraying the unparalleled splendor of the woman. The previous segment was brought to a close by means of the mention of Lebanon. The garden metaphor concludes in the same way.

The description of the motionless garden gives way to a rush of movement expressed in various verbal clauses. There are three imperatives addressed to the winds:

awake . . .

come . . .

blow . . .

and three jussives which appear to be expressing wishes:

let its fragrance waft . . .

let my beloved come . . .

let him eat. . . .

There is some dispute among commentators over the identity of the speaker in verse 16a. However, mention of "my garden" (v. 16b) clearly indicates that the man is speaking, and the reference to "his garden" (v. 16c) implies the woman. Since the three commands directed to the winds should be taken together, it seems clear that verse 16a is spoken by the man. The north and south winds would be cold and warm respectively. However, here the role of the winds is neither to cool nor to warm, but to spread the sensuous fragrances of the plants far and wide. They form a parallel pattern:

a   awake

b   north wind

a'   come

b'   south wind.

And they function as a merism (polar word pairs that include in their description everything between the poles as well as the poles themselves). Here the reference would be to all winds in general. Though the exotic spices and the woman they represent may be inaccessible, by means of the winds their and her extraordinary nature can be made known to all without risk of violation.

The second and third jussives in the second set of verbs ("let my beloved come . . . let him eat") are quite provocative. The jussive form itself places the verb somewhere between a wish and a command. The woman has been identified as the man's garden, enclosed and protected. However, she desires that he enter his garden and taste the exotic fruits that she has to offer him. Her words are clearly an expression of yearning, not only for his presence but also for the sexual intimacy that it promises.

The fulfillment of these desires is found in 5:1. It is clearly the man who speaks, using the garden metaphor as well as the double term of endearment that plays such an important role in this part of the unit, namely, "my sister-bride." Here again the very form of the verbs expresses the force of his statement. Using four verbs in perfect tense, he proclaims: I come, I gather, I eat, I drink. The objects of these verbs are the very intoxicating fruits of the garden: he gathers the myrrh with spice (4:14); he eats the honeycomb with the honey (4:11); he drinks wine with his milk (4:10b, 11b). These verbs, particularly "eat" and "drink," have strong sexual overtones. Throughout the Song of Songs, drinking wine has acted as a metaphor of making love. This is probably the case here as well. The longing has been assuaged; enjoyment of the beloved has become a reality. The extensive use of possessive pronouns throughout this verse (eight possessives in sixteen words) should be noted. This indicates that the man is appropriating everything to himself.

The voice that declares the last bicolon of verse 1 cannot be identified, and so over the years it has been interpreted in various ways. Most probably it is the man and woman who are being encouraged to eat, drink, and become intoxicated with love. Although linguistically this bicolon creates an abrupt shift in the poem, its repetition of some of the poem's significant words clearly creates links with it. The injunction to eat and drink follows immediately upon the man's exclamation of eating and drinking, and throughout the Song of Songs *dôdîm* carries the meaning of lovemaking. However this phrase is interpreted, it functions well as a conclusion for this particular segment, for the entire third part of the unit, and for the third unit of the Song of Songs.

ONE OF A KIND

(5:2–6:3)

The fourth unit of the Song of Songs (5:2–6:3) appears to be composed of two main parts, each with a refrain found elsewhere. More specifically it consists of an account of the woman's dream (5:2-7), which ends with the first refrain, an adjuration addressed to the daughters of Jerusalem (v. 8). This is followed by a dialogue between these same daughters and the woman, wherein they pose questions about her loved one (5:9; 6:1) and she responds (5:10-16; 6:2). The unit ends with a second refrain announcing the union of the lovers (v. 3). The previous unit focused on the beauty and desirability of the woman; this unit celebrates the incomparability of the man. It should be noted that sixteen of the thirty-two appearances of the term of endearment "my love" *(dôdî)* are found in this single unit. The word *dôdî*, along with the emphatic pronoun "I" *(ʾănî)* forms an inclusion within which the entire unit unfolds.

The first part of this fourth unit bears striking similarity to elements in the second unit (2:8–3:5). There the man approaches the house where the woman is to be found and he looks through the window (2:9); here he knocks on the door (5:2). In both places he calls to his beloved with words of endearment (2:10; 5:2); in both places she goes out into the city alone at night in search of him (3:2-3; 5:7). Finally, both passages close with an adjuration to the daughters of Jerusalem (3:5; 5:8).

Despite these similarities, the two passages are significantly different. The most obvious difference is seen in the way the searching-finding motif unfolds. In the former unit, after the man approaches the place where the woman is resting, she aggressively seeks him, finds him, embraces him, and eagerly takes him into the chamber of love. She adjures the daughters of Jerusalem not to interfere with their lovemaking. Here, it is because she hesitated in responding to the man that she must go out in search of him. She does not find him, and her adjuration to the daughters is an entreaty for their assistance. On this note the passage closes. Only at the end of the entire unit itself can any suggestion of union be found (6:3).

A Search at Night: 5:2-8

The first part of this unit consists of examples of the thematic patterns that give the Song of Songs its dynamic character: absence and presence, searching and finding. The man calls and the woman responds (vv. 2-6); the woman ventures out into the city in search of her love and the sentinels of the city react to her bold behavior (v. 7). The woman's search does not accomplish its end, and the adjuration to the daughters of Jerusalem that closes this first part of the unit elicits their help (v. 8). The emphatic pronoun "I" (*ʾănî*) both opens and closes this passage and accentuates four moments in the woman's longing for her beloved:

(v. 2)   I slept, but my heart was awake . . . my beloved is knocking

(v. 5)   I arose to open to my beloved

(v. 6)   I opened to my beloved

(v. 8)   . . . my beloved . . . I am faint with love[1]

These verbs—I slept, I arose, I opened, I am faint—characterize the experience of the woman, an experience of both longing and anticipation.

The poem begins with the woman stating that she was sleeping yet awake, an expression that only creates ambiguity and opens the passage to a variety of interpretations. Some commentators think that she is either dreaming,[2] in a state of semiwakefulness,[3] or merely fantasizing.[4] As we have already seen, the heart is the seat of thought rather than simply that of emotion. Therefore, we can say that the woman may be in some state of sleep, but her mind is awake. The participial forms of the verbs suggest that both sleep and wakefulness are states of some duration, rather than brief, intermittent moments. Actually there is little in what follows that corresponds to the typical dream narrative.

---

[1] See Carr, *Song of Solomon*, 131; Elliott, *Literary Unity*, 123–4.

[2] Gordis, *Song of Songs*, 62.

[3] Pope, *Song of Songs*, 511.

[4] Murphy, *Song of Songs*, 168.

In fact, the description of the episode with the sentinels in the city is quite realistic, suggesting that at least that incident could have really happened.[5]

The reference to sleep and wakefulness can probably be best understood as a poetic fiction that draws its images from both the world of dreams and the world of reality. Interpreting the opening phrase in this way recognizes the possibility of double entendre, while insistence on precise and consistent meaning tends to diminish the poetic force of the imagery used. Consequently, one can say that this is not a picture of a sleeping woman, awakened by the man's knocking on the door or window. Instead, she is in repose and alert at the same time. This is why she is able to call attention to the approach of her beloved *(dôdî)*, "Listen!" (see 2:8).

As was the case in 2:8, the Hebrew word *qôl* can be translated as the noun "voice" or as the interjection "hark!" or "listen!" Either translation of the word fits the context here. There is an insistence to the man's overtures. The Hebrew word for "knock" *(dôpēq)* denotes an energetic pushing rather than a gentle tapping.[6] Although such physical forcefulness does not fit the context of these love poems, the word does suggest the drive and energy of passion and loving desire itself. The man seeks entrance. His words are an imperative direct address. His entreaty is straightforward, but the meaning of his words is ambiguous: "Open to me." The word "open" is used three times in this passage (5:2c, 5a, 6a), never with a direct object, but always with *dôdî* as the indirect object. To what does he seek entrance? To her room? Or to the woman herself?

The names that the man uses in addressing the woman have become familiar terms of endearment. The possessive pronominal suffix of each indicates the bond that exists between him and the woman, and suggests that he does in fact have a right to be admitted. Each term of endearment denotes a particular aspect of the intimacy that the couple shares. "My sister" implies a permanent physical bond. Having been linked in other places in the Song of Songs with the bridal image (4:9, 10, 12; 5:1), it carries an added erotic connotation. "My love" refers to an intimate companion and is the man's most frequently used term of endearment (1:9, 15; 2:2, 10, 13; 4:1, 7; 6:4). "My dove" seems to be a pet name that characterizes the woman as the gentle bird that is associated with love itself (2:14). Finally, "my perfect one" is derived from the

---

[5] See Carr, *Song of Solomon*, 131–2; Fox, *Song of Songs*, 142; Snaith, *Song of Songs*, 71.

[6] Jacob is concerned that the flocks not be pushed beyond their endurance (Gen 33:13); the men of Gibeah pound on the door, demanding that the Levite be released to them (Judg 19:22).

Hebrew word meaning complete *(tām)*, and it suggests integrity and excellence. It could also refer to the woman's unblemished beauty or to her undivided commitment to the man she loves (6:9).

The reason given by the man for his need to be admitted is the dampness of his hair:

my head	is wet	with dew,
my locks		with the drops of the night

Presumably he has been out all night and his hair is now drenched with dew. Although the point of the image is the length of time that he has been waiting outside and not any thought of physical discomfort, one cannot deny how lame this reason sounds. The man almost appears to be whining. He has been waiting for a long time and he wants her to let him in. The woman's reply is in exact parallel form, providing two reasons for her hesitation in responding to his entreaty. However, her reasons sound as flimsy as were his motives for asking entrance:

I had put off	my garment;	how could I put it on?
I had bathed	my feet;	how could I soil them?

Her reply is puzzling. Throughout the poems she has longed for the man's presence and the intimacy that it promises. Here her words suggest that she is not only procrastinating, but she is ready for bed and she really does not want to be disturbed. She is actually considering forgoing a midnight rendezvous. Some interpreters understand the woman's response as a playful tease.[7] Others believe that she has been awakened from sleep, and she is bleary-eyed and confused.[8] Still others claim that she is merely musing within herself.[9]

This kind of complaint on the part of the man and the apparent reluctance of the woman to admit him do not easily fit the character of the mutually passionate love poetry found in the Song of Songs. However, Egyptian literature contains a form of poetry that is remarkably similar to this unusual feature. Known as a *paraclausithyron* ("beside an enclosure"), it describes a young man standing outside a girl's house, longing to get inside, and complaining because he is prevented from doing so.[10] In the previous poem examined above, the woman is described as an enclosed garden, a sealed fountain, inaccessible to all but the man she loves. Here she is enclosed once more, and it is up to her to

---

[7] See Gordis, *Song of Songs,* 62; Murphy, *Song of Songs,* 170.

[8] See Goulder, *Song of Fourteen Songs,* 41; Elliott, *Literary Unity,* 126–7.

[9] Falk, *Song of Songs,* 122.

[10] See Pope, *Song of Songs,* 522–4; Fox, *Song of Songs,* 282–3.

open to whomever she chooses. In the former poem she invited her lover into the garden. Will she do the same here? Her uncharacteristic behavior heightens the tension of the theme of longing.

This unusual call by the man and response of the woman can also be seen as a double entendre. The garment of which she speaks was a loose-fitting, ankle-length undergarment. In warm weather, it was often worn by itself but removed at bedtime. If she has taken it off, she is naked. For her to sleep like this would have been perfectly acceptable. However, to describe herself to the man as such would certainly be provocative. There is also a possible sexual allusion in her mention of washing her feet. While this was certainly a bedtime ritual, "feet" is also a common biblical euphemism for genitals (see 2 Sam 11:8, 11; Ruth 3:3-9; Isa 7:20). Since the eagerness with which the woman is always anticipating union with her lover precludes any thought of deliberate reluctance on her part, this unusual exchange could well reflect the influence of the *paraclausithyron*. The form itself heightens the absence-presence-absence motif and allows the poet to be sexually suggestive without being erotically explicit.

The woman's hesitation to open to the man does not prevent him from continuing his attempt to be united to her. In fact, it seems to encourage him to double his efforts. He seeks to open her door by inserting his hand into a lattice, or the latch or keyhole.[11] The Hebrew construction here is somewhat cryptic. The verb *(šālaḥ)* denotes forceful movement *toward* something, while the preposition *(min)* means "away *from*." This has led some interpreters to believe that the man is thrusting his hand into the opening, and others to maintain that he is withdrawing it. The forcefulness of his action, whichever direction it may be, corresponds with the forcefulness of his knocking on the door. The word "hand" *(yād)* is another double entendre with sexual connotations. Besides the obvious meaning, it has been used to refer to a memorial pillar that is rounded at the top (see 1 Sam 15:12; 2 Sam 18:18; Isa 56:5). In the ancient Near East this was clearly a phallic symbol. A second root, *ydd*, which means "to love," also yields the word *yād* and may be the basis for the reference to genitals (see Isa 57:8). Whichever origin the word might have, "hand" does carry sexual nuances.

The woman's reaction to the man's action is quite dramatic. Her innards, the seat of emotion (see Isa 16:11), are profoundly stirred for him. The word used here for innards or bowels *(mēʿeh)* also has sexual connotations. In a few instances it refers to the reproductive organs,

---

[11] A similar scene can be found in one ancient Egyptian love song, where the passionate man addresses the bolt of the door itself, asking to be admitted; Keel, *Song of Songs*, 190–1.

both male (see Gen 15:4[12] and female (see Ruth 1:11). It is also found in parallel construction with womb (*beṭer,* see Gen 25:23; Ps 71:6; Isa 49:1), thus reinforcing the sexual connotation. The double entendre is clear. The phrase can mean that the woman has been emotionally touched to the core of her being, or that the experience has aroused her sexually. However, to suggest that this verse is actually describing coitus is to ignore the details of the account that follows. It is only after the man forces his hand into the opening that the woman rises to open to him, and when she does open she finds that he has gone (vv. 5-6). Her rising makes no sense if thrusting his hand implies genital penetration and her stirring is an accompanying orgasmic response. Once again, this is a poetic description intended to suggest rather than to recount. It is nonetheless profoundly provocative.

The woman uses the emphatic pronoun "I" (*ʾănî*) to recount the fervor with which she finally rose to open to her beloved, a fervor that is in marked difference from her initial delay. The description of her hands is both sensual and puzzling:

my hands	dripped	with myrrh
my fingers		with liquid myrrh
		on the handles of the bolt

The image painted can be easily imagined. However, neither the origin of the myrrh, which in the Song of Songs always has erotic connotations (1:13; 3:6; 4:6, 14; 5:1), nor its purpose here can be easily determined. Did it come from the woman who, in preparation for a night of lovemaking, may have generously perfumed herself before retiring (see Prov 7:17)? If this is the case, then why did she resist rising immediately and opening when the man made his plea? Did the myrrh drop from the hand of the man when he thrust it through the latch hole in an effort to gain access to the woman? If so, why would a man who had been waiting all night have a hand so filled with myrrh that just touching the bolt would cause the woman's hand to drip with it?

Might this be yet another feature of the *paraclausithyron,* in which the dejected lover frequently left tokens of his love at the door that was closed to him? In some instances flowers were placed near the door, wine was spilled out in front of it, and perfume was poured on the door itself by disappointed lovers.[13] The ambiguity here allows for any

---

[12] The NRSV's "your very own issue" is, in the Hebrew, "one who will come forth from your *mēʿeh.*"

[13] Pope, *Song of Songs,* 522–3.

one of these interpretations. The myrrh could have come from the man, who was clearly anxious for an intimate encounter. It could have been carried by the woman, who was really eager for his company and was only teasing him with her delay. Most likely, if the origin of the myrrh were essential for understanding the passage, more detail would have been given. It is probably the presence of myrrh and the sensuous connotation that it carries that are important here.

The image of dripping or liquid myrrh adds to the sexual innuendo with which this passage is charged. We have already seen that "hands" is frequently a euphemism for genitals, male or female. Whether the myrrh comes from the man's hand or from the woman's hands, it could suggest the pungent yet appealing bodily fluids emitted during sexual arousal. Although the scene merely describes a visit of the man to the house of the woman, the images used in the description are particularly sexually suggestive.

Once again the woman uses the emphatic pronoun "I" (ʾănî) to recount her fervor (v. 5). In the previous verse, presumably she was filled with excitement and great anticipation as she prepared to open to her beloved. Here, when she finally does open to him, she is filled with disappointment and dismay. The repetition in close sequence of two verbs ("turned" and "gone") indicates the man's rapid departure and total disappearance. Has her rebuff angered him? Caused him to be dejected? Or, interpreting her delay and her response as a tease, is he now teasing her in return? The woman's disappointment at not finding him is acute (v. 6). She has lost an opportunity for a rendezvous with her lover, and she has no one to blame for this lost opportunity but herself. She is dispirited. Her emotional reaction makes her faint. The Hebrew states, "My soul went forth" (see Gen 35:18, where the death of Rachel is recounted). We today would say, "My heart sank" or "I nearly died."

There is some question about the reason for the woman's swoon. While the literal reading of the Hebrew (bĕdabbĕrô) yields "when he spoke," such a reading does not make sense, since the man has not spoken here. It would be more correct to say that she was overcome when she discovered that he had turned away and gone. A possible re-pointing of the Hebrew word could yield "because of him," a phrase that would make much more sense here.[14] There is also a root (dbr or dpr) in both Arabic and Akkadian languages that can be understood as "turn" or "flee." Such a change in vocalization offers a word that might throw light on the meaning intended here.[15] Her heart sank because

---

[14] Ibid., 525–6; *contra* Fox, *Song of Songs*, 145; Falk, *Song of Songs*, 184–5.

[15] Murphy, *Song of Songs*, 165.

he had gone. Using the same form that appeared in 3:1 the woman describes her immediate search for her lover and her failure to find him outside her door:

| I sought him, | but not | did I find him |
| I called him, | but not | did he answer |

It was this failure to find him near that prompted her to look for him elsewhere.

Once again the woman ventures out alone at night into the city in search of the man she loves (v. 7; see 3:2), and once again she encounters the sentinels as they make their rounds (see 3:3). In fact, the identical words are used in both instances. However, the two instances are significantly different. In the earlier passage she questioned the sentinels, but they did not respond. Here she does not speak to them, but they attack her. The reason for their fury is not given. Some commentators believe that they judge her to be a prostitute and respond accordingly. After all, she is in the city, the realm where only men or loose women are to be found; she is alone, conduct unbecoming decorous women in a patriarchal society; and it is night, the time when prostitutes frequently ply their trade. It would be easy to mistake her in this way.

The nature of the garment she was wearing *(rĕdîd)* may account for their mistake. This particular covering is only mentioned in one other place in the Bible, and there Isaiah lists it as an example of the superfluous finery of the daughters of Zion, finery that will be stripped from them by God because of their wanton behavior (cf. Isa 3:23). This is not just a night covering such as the one she took off as she readied herself for bed (v. 3). She may have thrown this garment on in haste; but it is an indication of luxury, and at night it could signify intended seduction (see Prov 7:10-12). According to Assyrian law, prostitutes wore no veils, and those who arrested them had the right to beat them and take their clothing. These customs might be behind what is otherwise a rather strange detail in this poem.

Not even the harsh treatment by the sentinels of the city can impede the woman from continuing her search for her lover. She turns next to the daughters of Jerusalem. She uses the same form of adjuration that she has used before (2:7; 3:5) and will use again (8:4) as she pleads for their help. However, in other poems, the adjuration includes *ʾim* ("if"), used in a negative sense. In those cases, the adjuration functions as a kind of oath, with which she implores that they not interfere with the natural unfolding of love. Here *ʾim* functions as a conditional conjunction and the adjuration is a simple yet heartfelt request that they intervene to speak on her behalf if they come across her lover.[16] They are asked to tell him of her intense longing for him, a longing that has overwhelmed her.

Once again the woman claims that she is "faint with love." Here too there is a difference in what this phrase implies. In the earlier passage (2:5), it was the pleasure that she enjoyed while in the arms of her lover that made her faint. Here her emotion is just the reverse; she is faint from longing for him. We see here how the context of the poem can produce a meaning quite different from that of the same words in a completely different context. The strength of the oath is depleted; the negative sense found in the other appearances of the adjuration is turned into a conditional request. The first part of this unit ends on a note of unfulfilled desire.

An Ode to His Body 5:9–6:3

The second part of the fourth unit is framed within a question-answer pattern. The daughters of Jerusalem ask the woman about the uniqueness of her beloved (*min* here in 5:9 means "more than" or "different from"),[17] and also about where he is to be found (6:1). She responds to the first query with a *waṣf* (5:10-16) and to the second with an answer that suggests the union of the lovers. The initial questioning takes the form of repetitive parallelism:

a   What (is)

b   your beloved

c   from other beloveds

d   Oh fairest among women

---

[16] This is contrary to Fox (*Song of Songs,* 146–7) and Snaith (*Song of Songs,* 76–7), who believe that all of the adjurations are negative statements. They maintain that the woman does not want her lover to know about her escapade into the city at night. This interpretation ignores the fact that she did not make this request in the adjuration that follows her description of the first time she ventured out.

[17] The same interrogative pattern—*mah* ("what"), a verb, *min* ("different from"), the inferior element in the comparison—is used in the well-known question asked during the Passover Haggadah: "How is this night different from all other nights?" Bloch and Bloch argue that the pattern differentiates rather than compares (*Song of Songs,* 184).

a'   What (is)

b'   your beloved

c'   from other beloveds

e   That you adjure us

Some commentators question whether the queries genuinely seek information about the identifying characteristics of the man or if they are meant to challenge the woman's insistence on his uniqueness.[18] Here and in the second questioning (6:1), the daughters refer to the woman with the same complimentary epithet used in an earlier poem by the man, "fairest among women" (1:8). Once again, it is not clear whether this is sincere flattery or subtle sarcasm. In either case, the use of the verb "adjure" links the questions posed by the daughters to the woman's adjuration in the previous poem. The questions themselves anticipate a response, as is found in what follows. Whatever the nature of the questioning, the woman takes it seriously and launches into an impressive description of her beloved's physical features.

Detailed descriptions of female physical beauty are quite common. Although they are rare, ancient Near Eastern literature does include a few comparable poems that admire men. However, these poems usually describe the man's physical strength or military accomplishments. Furthermore, we seldom find a record of an enamored woman employing a *waṣf* in celebrating the physical beauty of a man. The one found here is certainly the only example of its kind in the Bible.[19] The pattern of the poem is similar to an earlier *waṣf* with which the man praises the loveliness of the woman (compare 4:1-7). In both instances, the opening verse is a general statement that proclaims the subject's absolute beauty; the description then moves feature by feature from head to foot; the closing verse contains a summarizing statement about beauty generally. The opening and closing statements form a kind of inclusion. As a literary form, the inclusion itself suggests totality. The loved one, female or male, is totally and completely beautiful.

The *waṣfs* that describe the physical charms of the woman and of the man differ in interesting ways. In the earlier poem, the man spoke directly to the woman in first-person language. Here the woman speaks about him in third-person figurative description. The man employed imagery from the world of animals and vegetation. In addition to such imagery, the woman appeals to various natural features of gems and precious metals (compare Dan 2:31-33). One could say that the man's

[18] See Carr, *Song of Solomon*, 138–9; Keel, *Song of Songs*, 198.
[19] See Murphy, *Song of Songs*, 169; Fox, *Song of Songs*, 142.

imagination was captured by nature, while hers is inspired both by nature and by statues of gods with which she is familiar.[20] She seems to use the first kind of imagery to extol the beauty of the man's head and facial features, and the second kind to exemplify the splendor of the rest of his body.

The *waṣf* itself unfolds within an inclusion that is marked in two ways: both the opening verse and the one that closes it contain the word *dôdî*; both verses praise the man's extraordinary nature. The language employed in the *waṣf* is both graphic and hyperbolic. Proceeding from his head to his legs, the woman praises the color, the sweetness, the beauty, and the strength of the man's body. The expression with which the *waṣf* opens ("radiant and ruddy") is probably intended synecdochically to represent the total person and can be understood both descriptively and symbolically. The expression recalls the idealized characterization of the princes of Jerusalem (see Lam 4:7). The word for radiance *(ṣaḥ)* is rare and is used elsewhere to speak of the heat shimmering above the land (see Isa 18:4; Jer 4:11). Here the reference may suggest that the man both emanates radiance from within and resembles a luminous statue that reflects the brilliance of some external light. The man *(ʾādām)* is ruddy *(ʾādôm)*, a physical feature that suggests health and youthfulness (see 1 Sam 16:12; 17:42). Using the kind of hyperbole that marks the speech of lovers, the woman maintains that the good looks of the man she loves put him in a class apart from others.

The first three verses of the description (vv. 11-13) extol various features of the man's head. Two different words for gold are used to describe his head *(ketem* and *pāz)*. The combination of the two synonyms forms an asyndetic hendiadys translated "finest gold." This combination is not found elsewhere in the Bible, but similar constructions do appear (see Dan 10:5; 1 Kgs 10:18). The description is similar to that of the head of the statue that appeared in the dream of king Nebuchadnezzar (Dan 2:32). This characterization yields several different possible meanings, some of which conflict with other aspects of the poem. On the most basic level, gold may refer to the color of the man's skin, a tone that suggests health and beauty. However, the preceding verse states that he is ruddy, and so the reference to gold probably suggests something else. On another level, the resplendence of gold suggests the magnitude of the man's worth. Since this precious metal was used in the construction of images of royalty and gods, the metaphor might be conferring similar dignity on the man.

The word that describes the man's hair *(taltallîm)* is found nowhere else in the Bible. Basing the meaning of the word on Arabic cognates,

[20] Keel, *Song of Songs*, 202–4.

some believe that the reference is to the branches of a date palm. This would mean that the man's hair is thick.[21] Others rely on Mishnaic Hebrew, where the word means "wavy."[22] His hair is further compared to the black color of a raven. This blackness is in striking contrast to the gold of his head and the ruddiness of his complexion. These characterizations seem to conflict. However, we must remember that this is poetry and, understood from a presentational point of view, the imagery deliberately overstates in order to suggest the emotional reaction that the physical features of her lover awakened within the woman. Each depiction of a feature is independent of the rest. Together they constitute a kind of imagistic collage rather than a realistic portrait.

In two earlier poems the man declared that the woman's eyes are doves (1:15; 4:1). In those instances, the tenor of the metaphor was not given and so the comparison was open to various interpretations. In this poem it is the woman who compares the man's eyes with doves, and she includes an expansion of the description of the doves. This helps to focus the point of comparison. The doves are standing by springs of water (compare Joel 3:18 [MT 4:18]), washed in milk (compare Job 29:6), and fitly set. Each element in this threefold characterization provides a unique aspect to the comparison. The same Hebrew word (*ʿayin*) means both eyes and spring. The springs of water suggest the kind of abundance that is experienced only during the rainy season. The mention of milk might be a reference to the white color of the doves. However, bathing in milk also suggests lavishness. The exact meaning of the word translated "firmly set" (*millēʾt*) is uncertain. Since it is derived from the root for full (*mālēʾ*), it could be another suggestion of abundance. A related form describes a setting for jewels (see Exod 28:17). If this latter meaning is the one intended here, it suggests that the man's eyes were set in a brimming pool. All of the aspects of this description are somehow related to freshness, radiance and abundance.[23] Thus the metaphor seems to compare the moist milky-white doves with the glistening yet steady character of the man's loving eyes.

The woman next appeals to the intoxicating properties of certain fragrances as she continues her praise of the exceptional beauty of the man. As was the case with the visual metaphors, the comparisons here are hyperbolic overstatements of the kind that lovers use and they

---

[21] See Pope, *Song of Songs*, 536; Fox, *Song of Songs*, 147; Murphy, *Song of Songs*, 166; Keel, *Song of Songs*, 199; Bloch and Bloch, *Song of Songs*, 185.

[22] Snaith, *Song of Songs*, 80.

[23] The uncertain meaning of the Hebrew has led Murphy to suggest that "washed in milk" and "firmly set" refer to the man's teeth (*Song of Songs*, 166, 172). However, even he admits that there is no textual evidence for this emendation.

should not be forced into literal interpretations. The first reference is to cheeks, not whiskers as some commentators argue.[24] In an earlier poem the man had marveled at the beauty of the ornamentation of the woman's cheeks (1:10), now she marvels at the exhilarating scent of his. This verse appears differently in the Greek Septuagint from which we get the translation "yielding fragrances." However, the Hebrew has "towers of fragrances." This version calls to mind the Egyptian practice of placing cone-shaped headpieces made of aromatic substances on the heads of guests. So placed, the perfumed ointment would saturate the individual's hair, face, and upper body (compare Ps 133:2).

The verse contains a second metaphor that appeals to scent. Throughout the poems, various aspects of the lily have been employed in comparisons. Its beauty and singular delicacy have been ascribed to the woman (2:1, 2), and a bed of lilies has served as a symbol of the place of erotic repose (2:16; 4:5). Here the reference is to the extravagant aroma that ripened lilies release. This is an unusual image, because one would expect a metaphor of taste to describe the lips of a lover. However, as the woman's lips dripped honey, suggesting that her mouth overflows with delectability (4:11), the man's lips are said to drip myrrh, a resin with intoxicating qualities that always carry erotic meaning in the Song of Songs (1:13; 3:6; 4:6, 14; 5:1, 5). The point of the metaphor is certainly neither the taste of myrrh nor the scent of the man's lips, but the captivating nature of both. The man's lips are extolled less for their contour or color than for the enchantment that kissing them can generate.

In order to describe the man's arms, torso, and legs, the woman uses imagery that suggests statuary. The metaphors used follow the same pattern in each case. In the first colon, the body part is mentioned; this is followed by a noun in construct state; finally the precious substance is named. The second colon begins with a participle, followed by the name of a second precious substance:[25]

(v. 14a)	his arms	rolls of	gold		
(v. 14b)				set with	jewels
(v. 14c)	his belly	block of	ivory		
(v. 14d)				covered with	sapphires
(v. 15a)	his legs	columns of	alabaster		
(v. 15b)				set upon	bases of gold[26]

[24] Ibid., 166, 172; Keel, *Song of Songs*, 201.
[25] Translation based on NRSV, modified by the author.
[26] See Elliott, *Literary Unity*, 140.

The first metaphor is somewhat difficult to understand, since the Hebrew word *(yād)* is really "hand." However, the description of the rolls of gold does not fit this meaning well, unless the reference is to the man's fingers or arms. If this is the case, the image intended is of a bronzed man adorned with jeweled rings or armlets. There is ample evidence that ancient representations of gods were actually ornamented in this way. The grandeur of such statues and the value of the metals used in their construction and ornamentation made them apt vehicles for metaphors characterizing the man.

Moving further down his body, the woman marvels at the man's belly. The Hebrew word used *(mēʿeh)* usually denotes inner organs, bowels, even womb. The woman would not extol the man's belly unless it was naked, clearly a provocative thought. Although the precious gems probably refer to overlaid decoration, there might also be veiled allusion to the man's genitals. The generous use of double entendre throughout the poems leaves this reference open to such interpretation. The image depicted here recalls the statue in the dream of king Nebuchadnezzar (cf. Dan 2:32). In this *waṣf,* the man's belly is said to be like smooth ivory covered with sapphires or lapis lazuli. Perhaps the contrast between the ivory and the sapphire is meant to highlight the resplendence of the gem. In several places in the Bible, sapphire is associated with the deity. It is used of the pavement beneath God's feet (Exod 24:10); it is the composition of the divine throne itself (Ezek 1:26). Some kind of statue may have inspired this celebration of the man's torso.

The woman ends her praise of the physical features of the man with a consideration of his legs.[27] The mention of a solid base for his feet strengthens the idea of statuary. It should be noted that despite the obvious differences, both the man's head and his feet are made of the same precious metal. In other words, from head to foot, the man is as priceless as gold. There are no base elements in this image, no "clay feet" (compare Dan 2:33-34). The man is the embodiment of elegance, stature, and quality. Finally, his majesty, which consists of his height and strength and beauty and sweet smell, is compared to the magnificent cedars of Lebanon. With this final declaration of excellence, the *waṣf* is complete.

The woman concludes her description of the man with a comment about his mouth. The Hebrew word *ḥēk* refers both to the palate and to the organ of speech. The word suggests that her attention is not merely on his mouth, but on his open mouth, an image with sexual connotations. She states that his mouth is sweet (see Neh 8:10 where the word

[27] A similar metaphor is found describing the feet of a beautiful woman (Sir 26:18).

refers to sweet drink). Since in several other places in the Song of Songs the sweetness of taste is a reference to the sweetness of kisses (1:2; 2:3; 7:9 [MT 7:10]), it would seem appropriate to read this verse in that way as well. If his mouth is open, this would imply deep kissing. This is not to say that there is no allusion here to loving speech. It means, instead, that the passage should be interpreted in a way similar to the reading of an earlier one, where the man extols the woman's mouth for both its enticing speech and its passionate kisses (4:11). This reference to the man's sweetness forms the basis of his stated desirability.

This *waṣf* ends as it began, with a general statement about the extraordinary character of the man. He is both "distinguished among ten thousand" and "altogether desirable." This repetition reinforces the idea of the inclusion created by the word *dôdî*. The ending statement also parallels the ending of a *waṣf* proclaimed by the man:

(4:7)   you are altogether beautiful

(5:16)   he is altogether desirable.

The daughters of Jerusalem had asked: "What is your beloved more than another beloved?" Using the *waṣf*, the woman has answered their question. Her final words bring all aspects of her description to conclusion: This is who he is! The daughters challenged her, and she has more than met the challenge: "This is my beloved (*dôdî*) and this is my friend (*rēˁî*, the masculine form of *rēˁâ*, the word that the man uses for one of his terms of endearment in 1:9, 15; 2:2, 10, 13; 4:1, 7; 5:2; 6:4)."[28]

Once again the daughters question the woman regarding the man she loves. The pattern is the same as the one used in their earlier questioning (5:9); there is a twofold questioning, and the woman is addressed in the way the man refers to her:

Where   has he gone,   your beloved?

O fairest among women

Where   has he turned aside,   your beloved?

Most commentators believe that the woman's description of her beloved has so interested the daughters that they are willing to join her in her search. However, the last words of 6:1 need not imply that this is the case. The questions posed by the daughters could just as well express irony. They could imply that the man is not as eager for union as

---

[28] It should be noted that the word is traditionally translated "my friend" when referring to the man, but "my love" when referring to the woman. The reason for this disparity is unclear.

the woman is. If he is as committed to her as she is obviously committed to him, how does she explain his absence? Where has he gone? Where has he turned aside? From a literary point of view, the daughters play an important role in the movement of the Song of Songs. They function as a kind of sounding board. They provide an opportunity for the woman to express her longing and to declare her admiration and love. The text itself provides us with no more information about them than that.

The questions appear to be ironic in yet another way. Within this unit the woman has gone out alone into the city at night in search of her lover, but she has not found him. Furthermore, she has asked the daughters of Jerusalem to speak on her behalf if they happen to come upon him. It is obvious that the woman does not know where he is. Why then do they question her in this way? Even more puzzling, why does she answer in the way that she does? Once again we must remember that this is poetry, not logical prose. Furthermore, one of the primary undercurrents present in the Song of Songs is the absence-presence-absence motif. Like the first two units of the book, this fourth unit closes with the lovers united.

The woman's reply to the queries is rich in images found elsewhere in the poems. Chief among them are garden, spices, shepherding, flock, and lilies. Besides sketching a picture of profusion and tranquillity, they each carry connotations of erotic pleasure and satisfaction. The primary image is the garden. It is identified as belonging to the man. In an earlier poem, garden was used as a metaphor for the woman (4:12-16). She was initially described as a locked garden, but after she gave him access to the garden (4:16), it was referred to as "his garden" (4:16–5:1). The third unit of the Song of Songs closed with the man coming to his garden in order to enjoy the erotic pleasures that can be found there. This fourth unit closes in the same way.

The phrase "bed of spices," which is parallel to "his garden," is probably an allusion to the intoxicating nature of the woman whose charms were compared in earlier poems to exotic spices (4:10, 14; 5:1). The image of a bed suggests that the man can lie in the spices and luxuriate in their heady aroma. It is in the garden(s) that the man pastures his flock and gathers lilies (a variation of 2:16, where he pastures the flocks among the lilies). Since both garden and lilies have referred to the charms of the woman, and pasturing his flocks has referred to lovemaking (2:16), we can see how these images all allude to an anticipated intimate interlude for the lovers. This is confirmed by a declaration of mutual possession (v. 3; see 2:16 for the expression in reverse order). She is his, and he is hers. This simple yet passionate expression captures the essence of the entire Song of Songs. It describes total reciprocal self-giving and the acceptance by and of the other.

THE ADMIRATION OF A LOVER

(6:4–8:4)

The fifth unit is the longest one in the Song of Songs (6:4–8:4). Its limits are determined by two distinct refrains, "I am my beloved's and my beloved is mine" (6:3), which ends the previous unit, and "I adjure you, O daughters of Jerusalem" (8:4), which is the concluding statement of the fifth unit. The unit itself is a composite made up of words of admiration proclaimed by the man (6:4-10), a short statement by the woman (6:11-12), an address to the woman by unknown speakers along with her brief response (6:13 [MT 7:1]), more words of admiration by the man (7:1-9 [MT 7:2-10]), and two love monologues by the woman (7:10-13 [MT 7:11-14]; 8:1-4). Because of its length, there are many features in this unit that we have found in earlier units of the Song of Songs. There are questions and answers, sentiments of both heart-wrenching longing and delirious union, and metaphors taken from both nature and culture.

A Woman of Singular Beauty: 6:4-10

The man's words of admiration are framed within what might be called a double inclusion (6:4, 10). The most obvious feature of this inclusion is the repetition of the phrase "terrible as [an army] with banners" (vv. 4-7).[1] In addition to this feature, both verses contain imagery that, though quite different, may carry mythological connotations that have certain characteristics in common. The first few verses

---

[1] For various renditions of "banners" (*nidgālôt*) see Pope, *Song of Songs*, 560–3; Fox, *Song of Songs*, 152.

of this poem (vv. 4-7) form a *waṣf* that appears to be a shortened form of the one found earlier (4:1-7). Some of the details are identical in both cases; other details are specific to the respective poem. They begin with the same declaration of the woman's beauty (1:15; 4:1, 7). However, in the present poem her beauty is compared to the splendors of two prominent cities, Tirzah and Jerusalem.

Although characterizing a woman as a city is rare in the ancient Near Eastern world, the custom of portraying cities as females seems to have been a common practice. In some cultures, major cities were even personified as goddesses, the consorts of the local patron gods. Though this would not have been the practice in Israel, it is one of the possible mythological features behind the metaphor of the city used here. What may have been revered by others as a goddess has been demythologized by Israel. As splendid as the cities may have been, here they were only cities, and the extraordinary beauty of these demythologized cities is applied to the woman.

The first comparison is to Tirzah, the capital of the northern kingdom of Israel from the time of the reign of Jeroboam to that of Omri (ca. 930–880 B.C.E.);[2] the second comparison is to Jerusalem, the capital of the southern kingdom of Judah. Like those proud cities, the woman possesses regal demeanor and extravagant splendor. Being capital cities, they would certainly be protected by thick surrounding walls. Cities whose walls had not been violated by enemies were considered "virgin" cities. The metaphor of such a walled city has certain features in common with an enclosed garden and a sealed fountain, two metaphors that have already been used to describe the woman (4:12). In the earlier *waṣf*, the walls and towers of a fortified city were applied to the woman (4:4); in this poem, her beauty is compared to the fortified cities themselves.

The Hebrew text mentions awe-inspiring *(ʾăyummâ)* banners, but not an army. In another place in the Bible (see Hab 1:7), a form of the adjective suggests a military image. For this reason, many translators include the word "army" in this passage as well. Using such military imagery to describe a woman may seem strange, even offensive, to the contemporary reader. However, in order to concretize his praise, the man simply chose realities from his own experience, realities that were renowned for their commanding splendor. Furthermore, in the ancient world the goddess of love was often also the goddess of war. Examples of this include the Assyrian Ishtar, the Greek Aphrodite, and the Hindu

---

[2] The reason why Tirzah is cited rather than Samaria, which was the northern capital for almost 160 years, may be the similarity between the name Tirzah and *rāṣâ*, the Hebrew verb which means "to be pleased with."

Kali. The point of the reference here is the appeal of the woman's physical features. She is beautiful and awe-inspiring.

The closing verse of the inclusion begins with a question, "Who is this?" This is the same stylized formula found in the description of the wondrous procession coming out of the wilderness (3:6). Here the comparison is with the marvelous heavenly bodies. The dawn or morning star was a divine being in Canaanite mythology. The words *lĕbānâ* (white) and *ḥammâ* (heat) are poetic ways of speaking of the moon and the sun respectively (see Isa 24:23; 30:26). The phrase "terrifying as [an army with] banners," applied here to the heavenly bodies rather than to the capital cities, is probably an allusion to the stars, known as the "hosts of heaven" (see Deut 17:3). Once again, the context suggests a military allusion. Just as with references to Tirzah and Jerusalem (v. 4), where the phrase suggests the military banners of a fortified city, so here it suggests a cosmic army. In the ancient Near Eastern world, these celestial beings were universally revered as deities. The warlike Ishtar, surrounded by stars, was frequently accompanied by the sun and the moon.[3] Though Israel demythologized these heavenly bodies, they were still considered marvels. To characterize the woman in this way was to accord her the highest praise. In the eyes of the man who loves her, she is as awe-inspiring as the beautiful capital cities and the resplendent celestial bodies, all of which carry traces of divinity.

Within this inclusion the admiration of the man is expressed through two different forms. The *waṣf* (vv. 5-7) is spoken directly to the woman; a boasting song is spoken about her (vv. 8-9). The order of the elements of praise within the *waṣf* is the same as that found in the earlier, parallel *waṣf* (4:1-3). The man's attention is drawn first to the woman's eyes, then to her hair, her teeth and her cheeks (reference to her lips is omitted here).

The man's tribute to the woman's eyes is markedly different from that found in the first *waṣf*. There the man cries out in delight, characterizing her eyes as doves (4:1); here he acknowledges the fearful effect they have on him, and he implores her to turn her eyes away from him. There seems to be a gradual intensification in the power that the woman's eyes exert over the man. First they are calming, reminding him of the gentleness of the doves (4:1). Then they ravish his heart (4:9). Here they overwhelm him. While it may seem incongruous to some, the connection between beauty and terror is well attested in romantic literature.[4] This request is not to be taken seriously, for the man clearly desires to be overwhelmed by her. This is the way lovers talk. The

[3] Keel, *Song of Songs*, 220–1.
[4] Landy, *Paradoxes of Paradise*, 137–79.

description of her eyes is consistent with the man's allusion to her
awe-inspiring character. The presentational character of his metaphoric
language is obvious.

The rest of the *waṣf* is identical to the earlier one. Except for the
omission of *har* ("mountain"), the man's comparison of the woman's
flowing black hair to a flock of goats repeats what is found in 4:1. There
is also only one slight difference in the reference to her white teeth. In
the first *waṣf* the flock consists of sheep that have been shorn; in the
second it is made up of ewes, but there is no mention of shearing. There
are no differences in the characterization of her cheeks, which flush
with the color of the pomegranate. (For a careful analysis of the elements of this *waṣf*, see the commentary on 4:1-3).

The boasting song (vv. 8-9) reintroduces the royal fiction found in so
many places in the Song of Songs, particularly the description of
Solomon's procession (3:6-11). The earlier poem spoke of sixty mighty
men (3:7); this one speaks of sixty royal women (6:8-9). Mothers are
prominent in both poems: in the first poem Solomon is crowned by his
mother (3:11), and the beloved woman of this poem is favored by hers
(6:9). The classifications of women reflect the social categories present
in the royal harems of the ancient Near East. First there were the official
wives, then the concubines, and finally the court maidens who served
the wives and concubines. In the midst of all of these royal women, the
man's loved one is unique, one of a kind (*ʾaḥat*, v. 9). By tracing a sequence of increasing numbers—sixty, eighty, countless—the man is
underscoring the limitless superiority of the woman he loves, another
way of illustrating her uniqueness. Even collectively the other women
cannot compare with her. There is distinct pride in the man's boasting.

The man's description of his love includes two of the terms of endearment that he used when he called to her to open to him: "my dove,
my perfect one" (5:2). Here he links his own adulation to the favor in
which her mother holds her:[5]

unique	is she	to her mother
darling[6]	is she	to the one who bore her

Her uniqueness does not mean that she was an only child. Rather, it denotes the singular affection that her mother has toward her. In other
words, even within her own family she is in a class by herself. Once
again attention turns to the queens and concubines. This time "daugh-

---

[5] Author's translation.

[6] The Hebrew *bārâ* can be translated in various ways: "pure," "clean," "chosen."
The same word modifies sun (v. 10).

ters" is substituted for "maidens." Three verbs report the reaction of the women of the court toward the woman of the Song of Songs: they saw her, they called her happy, they praised her. The Hebrew word translated "praise" *(hālal)* also yields "boast." Thus, the poem is a boasting song of the man, and it recounts the boasting of the courtly women.

Signs of Spring: 6:11-12

This short passage is very difficult to translate and to interpret.[7] The identity of the speaker is a disputed point. Some claim that it is the man, since throughout the earlier poems, the woman is the one who is characterized as a garden (4:12, 16). It is to her that the man goes seeking entrance (4:16; 5:1; 6:2).[8] However, in an upcoming poem (7:11-13 [MT 7:12-14]), it is the woman, using the same uncommon language as found here ("budded" and "in bloom," 6:11; 7:12 [MT 7:13]), who invites the man into the fields to see the blossoming of spring. This has led other commentators to maintain that it is the woman who is speaking here as well.[9]

This is the only place where the word for nut *(ʾĕgôz)* appears and so its precise meaning cannot be discerned for sure. However, its frequent use later in Rabbinic literature helps us to identify it as a walnut. In ancient Near Eastern mythology, the nut was thought to possess both magical and sexual properties, just as vines and pomegranates do in the Song of Songs.[10] Thus, whatever the exact meaning of this reference may be, its exotic and erotic character is unmistakable. The valley *(naḥal)* is really a wadi, a dry river bed that can become a raging torrent during the rainy season. At that time of the year a profusion of flowers seems miraculously to appear in what is otherwise a wilderness. Because of the sudden and extravagant explosion of lush vegetation, these were often places where fertility worship was practiced (see Isa 57:6). The blossom of the valley *(ʾēb)*[11] is the kind of flower that flourishes for only a short period of time. Even with water it withers before any other plant. The woman says that she went to the garden to see

[7] For various readings see Pope, *Song of Songs*, 92.

[8] See Elliott, *Literary Unity*, 159–62; Bloch and Bloch, *Song of Songs*, 192.

[9] See Fox, *Song of Songs*, 155; Murphy, *Song of Songs*, 178–9; Snaith, *Song of Songs*, 94–5.

[10] Pope, *Song of Songs*, 574–9.

[11] The word appears elsewhere only in Job 8:12.

these blossoms as well as the budding vineyard. The references are to springtime, to the time of burgeoning life, a fit image for the promise of new yet unfulfilled love. Like the short lifetime of the blossom of the valley, the opportune time for a tryst may be but a fleeting moment and so the lovers will have to take advantage of it when it comes.

The next verse (v. 12) is considered the most difficult in the entire Song of Songs. As it stands, the Hebrew is unintelligible. Most interpreters emend the text, thereby determining its meaning rather than discovering it.[12] This verse is usually attributed to the same speaker as the previous verse, either the woman (the position held here) or the man.[13] The verse itself begins with an expression that describes the speaker as being taken by surprise. Before she knew it, the woman was transported to the chariot of a nobleman. This image corresponds to an earlier one, where reference to the litter of Solomon contributes to the royal fiction employed in the Song of Songs (3:7). Both the litter and the chariot are majestic vehicles of transportation, vehicles that provide ample opportunity for the passengers to engage in lovemaking.

An Ode to the Dancer: 6:13–7:5 [MT 7:1-6][14]

Once again the man employs a *waṣf* to describe some of the physical features of the woman he loves. The introductory verse of this *waṣf* yields several interpretations, all of which depend upon how the preceding passage was understood. The first word *(šûb)* can be translated "turn"[15] or "return."[16] If the woman went down to the nut garden in the previous passage (6:11), she could be called upon here to "return." Or, if she was taken by surprise (v. 12), it could be that she is called upon

[12] For a discussion of the various interpretations see Pope, *Song of Songs*, 584–92.

[13] Keel believes that v. 11 is spoken by the man, but v. 12 by the woman (*Song of Songs*, 225).

[14] The Masoretic Text (that is, the standard edition of the Hebrew Bible, abbreviated "MT") begins ch. 7 at this point. However, many English translations follow the numeration of the ancient Greek translation, the Septuagint, which numbers the first verse of this passage 6:13 and begins numbering ch. 7 with the next verse. Throughout ch. 7, therefore, the verse numbers of the Hebrew Bible are one higher than those of most English translations. We will follow the numbering of the NRSV, and indicate the higher Hebrew numbers in brackets in the headings.

[15] See Gordis, *Song of Songs*, 95; Elliott, *Literary Unity*, 162–3; Murphy, *Song of Songs*, 181. Pope has "leap" (*Song of Songs*, 595).

[16] See Fox, *Song of Songs*, 157; Goulder, *Song of Fourteen Songs*, 55; Keel, *Song of Songs*, 228; Snaith, *Song of Songs*, 97–8.

here to return to her senses. The theme of dance, which follows this vocative expression, and the rhythmic impression produced by the fourfold repetition of *šûb*, suggest that the word could also be translated "turn."

The identity of the Shulamite has also perplexed interpreters. Is this reference an allusion to Shunem, the Jezreelite village from which came Abishag, the wife of David whose possible future with Adonijah threatened the sovereignty of King Solomon (1 Kgs 2:13-25)? This interpretation would give historical mooring to the Song of Songs. Is the word a form of Shulmānîtu, the name of a Mesopotamian goddess of war? This view would support the mythological and military imagery that some translations favor. Or is the term merely a derivation of *šlm*, the Hebrew root from which come the names Solomon and Jerusalem and the word peace *(šālôm)*?[17] This latter explanation, where the name characterizes the woman as a female counterpart of the fictional Solomon, appears to be the most likely one. This view brings together all three aspects of the word *šlm*. It accounts for the Solomonic fiction, the frequent references to Jerusalem, and the description of idyllic or peaceful settings.

A third ambiguous feature of these verses is the identity of the speaker. The pronouns here and in the response that follows are plural, and so this cannot be a short exchange between the man and the woman. The Hebrew verb for "look upon" *(ḥāzâ)* seldom refers to simple perception. It signifies a look of remarkable intensity, the kind of look inspired by an object of sight that is considered an exalted vision. Whoever is speaking to the woman is desirous of beholding her extraordinary appearance, whether that be the way she looks or the way she acts. She replies to their request, Why do you want to look upon me? This cannot be the response of a naive maiden who is unaware of her beauty, for she herself attested to it earlier (1:5). Does her demure response originate from a sense of propriety that might allow her to expose herself to her lover but certainly not to the general public? The meaning of this phrase hinges on the character of the dance. What kind of dance is meant? The Hebrew word *(maḥănāyim)* is in dual form, indicating a pair of something, but of what? two armies? two dancers? two spectators? The word has been understood in various ways.

The *waṣf* itself (7:1-5), which is similar to the two earlier *waṣf* (4:1-7; 5:10-16) and which clearly explains why anyone would want to look at the woman, graphically describes various parts of her body in an orderly

---

[17] For a summary of the various interpretations, see Pope, *Song of Songs*, 596-600. Fox translates it "perfect one" (*Song of Songs*, 157–8).

sequence. While the sequence in the other poems moved downward, the description in this poem begins with the woman's feet and moves upward to her head. This change in direction may result from the attention that was caught by the woman's dancing feet. From there, the man's gaze moves up her body. As was the case with the previous *waṣfs*, some of the comparisons are similes, using the comparative particle "like" *(kĕ)*, others are metaphors that, for the sake of forceful description, apply some characteristic to one of the woman's physical features. Finally, besides employing well-defined imagery to describe the woman's physical features, the vocabulary used carries clear though secondary sexual connotations.

The man begins his song of praise of the woman by extolling the beauty of her feet. This is not the usual word for foot *(regel)*, which is frequently used as a euphemism for genitalia. Instead, it is the word that can be translated "footstep" or "anvil" *(paʿam)*, a word that suggests the sound rather than the appearance of the foot. This draws attention to the sound of the sandaled foot, rather than to its appearance. Rural women and professional dancers normally went barefoot. Sandals were considered a decorative or sophisticated addition, more easily available to women of noble or upper-class status (see Ezek 16:10; Jdt 10:4). This feature, along with the fact that the woman is called "daughter of a noble," furthers the royal fiction that is so prevalent in the Song of Songs and that connotes the exceptional character of this woman. Were she really a member of the nobility, she would probably not be dancing in public. Sandals were often considered quite beguiling. The sandals of the Jewish heroine Judith were said to have ravished the eyes of the Assyrian general Holofernes (cf. Jdt 16:9). In this poem of admiration they denote not only movement, rhythm, and perhaps even sound, but also allurement.

The form of most of the comparisons in this *waṣf* is consistent. A part of the body, the referent of the metaphor, is named first. This is followed by mention of the vehicle of the comparison, along with the descriptive addition of a particular feature of that vehicle. This feature is not ascribed to the female body part but is an attribute of the vehicle, enhancing its own significance. Only indirectly is it applied to the woman. In other words, the jewelry, not the woman's thighs, is the handiwork of the artisan; the rounded bowl, not her navel, never lacks mixed wine; the wheat, not her belly, is encircled with lilies; the fawns, not her breasts, are the twins of the gazelle. Nonetheless, these embellishments make the vehicles of the metaphors even more appealing comparisons of the woman's charms.

After the woman's feet, the feature that catches the man's eye is her thighs. Mention of this body part is frequently found in passages describing how people would touch the thigh and swear an oath (see Gen 24:2, 9; 47:29). Since it is the genitalia and not the thigh that is the source of life, it was certainly these sexual organs that were touched and the reference was probably used in this way as a euphemism. In patriarchal societies, such oaths were made "under the thigh" of men and not of women, and so this would not be the sense in which the word is used here. However, the thigh is still a part of the body that carries sensuous, if not sexual, connotations.

The actual description of her thighs (v. 2) contains three words found nowhere else in the Bible: the adjective ("turning"; NRSV, "rounded") used in the description of her thighs, the jewelry to which her thighs are compared, and the artisan who crafted the jewels. These unusual words make precise interpretation of the metaphor quite difficult. The first *hapax legomenon*,[18] the describing adjective, can refer to curvaceous shape or sinuous movement. If the first meaning is intended, the reference could be to the woman's buttocks, the part of the lower thigh that is particularly rounded; if the second meaning is intended, it could imply that her upper thighs are undulating in some kind of sensuous dance. The jewelry, the second *hapax*,[19] the vehicle to which her thighs are compared, could be an allusion to an ornamental ringed belt that women wore suspended around their hips. This kind of ornamentation flowed and waved and, perhaps, shimmered with the swaying that is part of the dance. Such motion and glitter would certainly catch the fancy of those watching the woman's movements. Finally, although *ʾommān* ("artisan") is a *hapax*, it is clearly a reference to the skillful hand that crafted the jewelry. This last feature indicates the artistic character of the jewelry, which, through the instrumentality of the metaphor, is transferred to the thighs of the woman. They too are exquisitely fashioned.

The roundness of the woman's body continues to hold the attention of the man as his eyes move to her navel and her belly. Because the description moves upward and the navel is above not beneath the belly, which is also extolled later in this poem, some commentators maintain that the reference here is to the vulva.[20] However, strict adherence to the actual structure of the body is really not observed in *waṣfs*, as we

---

[18] A *hapax legomenon* is a word that appears only once in the Bible. Its uniqueness means that we have no other contexts from which to infer its meaning, and that often makes translation and interpretation conjectural.

[19] The singular form of this word is used elsewhere with *nezem*, a word that means ornamental ring (Prov 25:12; Hos 2:13 [MT 2:15]).

[20] See Pope, *Song of Songs*, 617; Keel, *Song of Songs*, 234; Murphy, *Song of Songs*, 182, 185; Snaith, *Song of Songs*, 101–2.

will see later in this poem when the description of the woman's eyes precedes that of her nose (v. 4). Therefore, emendation of the text for the sake of strict ordering does not seem to be necessary here. Exposing the navel was then and continues today to be very provocative, and this practice serves the awe-inspiring purpose of the *waṣf*. Pressed into the body, the navel would take on a concave shape, rounded *(hapax)* like a vessel that held an exotic mixture *(hapax)*. The exotic mixture denotes the extraordinary character of the rounded bowl, not the navel of the woman. This rounded bowl is not a common vessel used for everyday purposes; it is special. Since the umbilical cord was the original source of nourishment, the navel has always retained this connection with life and sensuality.

The man's admiring gaze is next fixed on the woman's belly *(beṭer)*, which is compared to wheat. The basic meaning of the word is "interior," thus lending itself to the translation "womb" as well as "belly." However, as employed here, the reference must be to some external feature of the belly, otherwise the man would not have been entranced by its beauty. The descriptive phrase that modifies the vehicle might throw some light on the point of comparison intended in this metaphor. It was the practice to leave the cut wheat in piles in the fields. This practice may lie behind the image here. However, is the point of comparison the roundness of the heaps? The tawny color of the wheat? And what might the encirclement of the lilies imply? Another harvest practice was the bundling of the wheat. In order that the piled wheat not be blown away or eaten by roaming animals, it was frequently protected by a hedge of thorns or thistles. Might the circle of lilies be an allusion to this practice? Finally, since wheat is a staple of life, and the wheat described here is ripened and harvested and possesses the potential for nourishing, the metaphor also carries the notion of fecundity and sustenance. But again, which characteristic is the intended tenor of this metaphor? It may be that the poet wanted all of these characteristics to be operative, thus according a multifaceted comparison to the woman's belly.

In words identical to those found in an earlier *waṣf* (4:5), the woman's breasts are next compared to twin fawns of the gazelle, an animal renowned for its grace and beauty, and whose name comes from the Hebrew word *(ṣĕbî)* meaning splendor or glory (see Isa 4:2; 28:5).[21] The fawns suggest youthfulness and all of the comeliness that accompanies

---

[21] The phrase "that feeds among the lilies," found in 4:5, is omitted here, probably in order to preserve the structure found in the earlier verses of the *waṣf*. This structure consists of a mention of the part of the woman's body, the identification of the vehicle of the metaphor, and a single phrase that describes the vehicle.

it. The woman's breasts are like these fawns, which have all of the comeliness of youth along with the grace and beauty associated with the gazelle. The characterizations of the woman's thighs, navel, belly, and breasts all indicate that much of her body can be clearly seen. It is unlikely that she is naked, since that would be out of character for the kind of woman that elsewhere in the Song of Songs she is portrayed to be. Perhaps she is wearing a diaphanous veil-like garment, which would allow the contours of her body to be seen through its cover. Though a covering, such a garment would be quite revealing and thus provocative. While respectable women would probably not dress like this in public, it might be a typical way of dressing during some kind of dance.

The characterization of the woman's neck is the only element in this *waṣf* that does not follow the pattern identified earlier. It is a simple metaphor with a referent (neck), the comparative particle "like" *(kĕ)*, and a vehicle (tower). Some scholars believe that originally there was a modifying phrase that has been lost or misplaced.[22] On the other hand, the metaphor itself may have been added as an afterthought, for in the very same verse, the woman's nose is also compared to a tower. Whatever the case, the metaphor itself is striking. In an earlier poem, the woman's neck was compared to the tower of David built of squared stone blocks and adorned with military trappings (4:4). Here it is likened to an ivory tower. The image suggests a long, stately neck. In one of the opening poems of the Song of Songs the woman commented on her dark coloring (1:5), and so here ivory is probably a reference to extraordinary value rather than to a creamy complexion. In the *waṣf* that extolled the splendor of the man's body, the woman compared his torso to ivory (5:14). Here he returns the compliment.

Throughout the poem, eyes are usually compared to doves (1:15; 4:1; 5:12), gentle birds that symbolize love. Here they are likened to pools of water. This is an understandable comparison, since the Hebrew word *ʿayin* means both "eye" and "water source." The metaphor suggests water that is tranquil, not flowing as spring water would be. Heshbon was an Amorite royal city east of Jerusalem in the modern country of Jordan. Recent excavations there have unearthed the remains of huge reservoirs of remarkable masonry, which probably held the water supply for this city renowned for its abounding fertility and rich vineyards. Like Tirzah and Jerusalem, the other cities mentioned in the description of the woman (6:2), Heshbon's inclusion here furthers the royal fiction seen so frequently in the Song of Songs. The woman's eyes are not compared to just any pools of water, but to famous pools in

[22] See Fox, *Song of Songs*, 158; Murphy, *Song of Songs*, 182.

a royal city. The pools represent water that is deep and mysterious. When applied to the woman's eyes, the image is quite provocative.

The gate is called Bath-rabbim, literally "daughter of many." The actual site is unknown, but the name itself suggests an interesting interpretation. In ancient cities, gates were frequently named for the town or village toward which they opened. (Jerusalem itself boasts the Jaffa Gate and the Damascus Gate.) The gate in this poem might well have opened toward Bath-rabbim. Furthermore, just as cities were generally characterized as feminine, so the surrounding villages that were dependent upon these cities were frequently referred to as daughters. The gate closest to the water supply, which provided water for the city itself as well as for the surrounding villages, would most likely be the busiest gate of the city. Therefore, it could have been called the "gate of the daughter of many." This image of the openness of the pools of Heshbon to refresh all those who approach the gate is applied to the eyes of the woman. They too are deep and open for the refreshment of others.

The woman's nose is next compared to a tower of Lebanon. The image may strike modern sensitivities as strange and even offensive, because in the ancient world as in that of today, a long nose was not considered particularly attractive. However, it should be noted that each time the word "tower" has been used in a comparison of some physical feature of the woman, its primary focus has been something other than height. When her neck was likened to the tower of David (4:4), the point of comparison was the adornment that it displayed. This suggested that the woman was also elaborately adorned. When it is compared to a tower of ivory (7:4), it is probably the stateliness of the tower and its value that are points of comparison. All of this notwithstanding, this particular metaphor has been very difficult to interpret.

Although the nose is the organ of scent and Lebanon (*lĕbānôn*) is closely connected to frankincense (*lĕbônâ*), the point of comparison here is probably less that of fragrance than something about the mountain itself. Besides the similarity in the sound of the two words, both Lebanon and frankincense share the same color: the cliffs of the Anti-Lebanon mountain range are chalk-colored and frankincense is white. This color connection may in fact be the reason for the linguistic correspondence. Finally, it is not clear whether the reference here is to an actual tower built on a mountain peak, to the mountain range itself, or to one of the peaks of that range. Since the metaphor that follows this one includes a reference to Carmel, a mountain, "tower of Lebanon" is understood here as a particular promontory of the mountain range.[23]

[23] Some commentators believe that this is a veiled reference to Mount Hermon; see Murphy, *Song of Songs*, 183.

The promontories of the Anti-Lebanon mountain range fall steeply down to the major road that leads to Damascus. Any one of these headlands would certainly command attention and respect. It would be a place from which one could survey a panoramic scene. The point of comparison might be the privileged position that such a promontory provides as well as the straight descent from the mountain itself to the road. The metaphor characterizes the woman's nose as long and straight; its bridge is connected to the woman's eyes, which have command over her surroundings.

The final metaphor of this *waṣf* compares the woman's hair with a feature of Mount Carmel, one of the most majestic elevations in the north of Israel. Though it cannot rival the heights of the Anti-Lebanon range, Carmel has an imposing appearance, rising abruptly out of the Plain of Esdraelon and jutting into the Mediterranean Sea. This mountain was not a barren crag, but a heavily wooded area with dense vegetation. The metaphor suggests that just as Mount Carmel rose dramatically above its surroundings, so the woman's head with its captivating tresses was a fitting crown proudly placed above the rest of her body. The similarity between the name of the mountain *(karmel)* and the word for scarlet *(karmîl)* has been noted by most commentators. Besides being linked with the promontory in Lebanon mentioned in the previous verse, the paronomasia links this mountain with the next phrase in the poem, which characterizes the woman's hair as purple.

This hair coloring has puzzled commentators. Was the woman's hair actually dyed purple? Or was this a reference to its sheen as it caught the light? The designation purple *(ʾargāmā)* includes all shades of the color from violet to deep blue-black. Symbolically it is associated with royalty and the gods. The color itself was most likely obtained from a secretion of a gland in the stomach lining of the murex shellfish, a sea creature found in abundance on the Mediterranean coast. This coloring provided various names for the vicinity. Besides Carmel itself, Canaan means "land of purple" and Phoenicia comes from the Greek word for "red-purple." In this description, two words are used for hair: *dallâ,* from the verb for "hang down" (like threads that dangle from a weaver's loom; see Isa 38:12), and *rĕhāṭîm,* from the verb for "run," suggesting a rippling effect. In earlier poems the woman's hair was compared to a flock of black goats streaming down the slopes of Gilead (4:1; 6:5). Here the image is of the troughs into which water flows for the watering of the flocks. Though this metaphor is quite different from the earlier one, the tenors of the comparisons are the same. The woman's hair is deep-colored, long, and flowing.

The final phrase of this verse is difficult to interpret. It departs from the description of the woman and moves to a report of her effect on the man. The image that is generated is curious. The Hebrew states that a king, most likely the man of the Song of Songs, is trapped in conduits or watercourses (rĕhāṭîm), presumably her flowing hair. Mention of a king is probably another example of the royal fiction. As always, it emphasizes the extraordinary character of the major players in this romantic drama. In other words, the man is held captive by the radiance and seductive appearance of the woman's hair. Just as the _waṣf_ opened with a declaration of her queenly nature, it closes characterizing him as a king.

Although they are used for poetic force, the geographic references in this _waṣf_ cannot be overlooked. Heshbon, Lebanon, Damascus and Carmel are all situated on or near one of the important international highways that traversed the land of Israel. Heshbon was located where the King's Highway passed to the north to Phoenicia. A second road, the Via Maris, wound its way around Mount Carmel, passing the Anti-Lebanon and Lebanon ranges on its way to Damascus. Along such travel routes came the caravans carrying the spices, precious metals, and rich dyes referred to in many of the poems of the Song of Songs. All of these features demonstrate the international character of the poems, as well as the universally recognized beauty of the woman.

The Desires of Love: 7:6-9a [MT 7:7-10a]

The song of admiration (7:6-9a) begins with an exclamation of praise, "How beautiful and how pleasant!" This double adjectival exclamation, accepted by most commentators, is followed by a phrase that has been interpreted in various ways. Some read it as a double vocative addressed to the woman, "loved one, delightful one." Because the Hebrew word ʾahăbâ is an abstract form of the verb "to love," others believe that love itself is being addressed and lauded. The second term of address is also variously rendered "daughter of delights," "delightful daughter" or simply "delight." Because the ensuing poem describes the physical delights that the woman's body provides and which the man hopes to enjoy, other interpreters maintain that, instead of being terms of endearment addressed to the woman, the words "love" and "delight" refer to the pleasures of lovemaking. Even with these slight differences, most maintain that the celebration of the woman's beauty found in the preceding _waṣf_ now moves into anticipation of enjoying the delights that her alluring body can afford.

In the previous _waṣf_ the man's appreciative glance traveled the entire height of the woman from her feet to her head. It is fitting then that in the song of admiration that follows he should use the metaphor of a tree to praise her desirability. Similar comparisons to trees have already appeared in earlier poems. The woman compared her loved one to an apple tree that provided both shade and the taste of sweetness (2:3), as well as to a cedar of Lebanon, a tree renowned for its firmness and enduring character (5:15). Here the tree that he chooses to describe her is the date palm, a tree that in various cultures represented grace and elegance and whose huge date clusters resemble female breasts. Because its abundant fruit was a source of nourishment, the date palm also came to symbolize the tree of life. The fruit of the date palm was produced high above its tall stately trunk, making it relatively inaccessible, another image of the reclusive disposition of the woman. This image suggests that both the fruit of the tree and the breasts of the woman are mature and enticing.

The inaccessibility of the woman's charms does not deter the passionate man. He will climb the palm tree and harvest its fruit. The sexual allusions to climbing the woman are obvious. Verse 8 alludes to three different harvest periods—dates in August, grapes from August to September, apples during autumn. Although earlier the love shared by the woman and the man is described as fresh and youthful as springtime (2:11-13), the maturity of the couple, at least of the woman, is clear from the use of harvest imagery. This imagery is certainly erotic. The woman's sexually developed body does not seem to be desired by the man for the sake of reproduction, but for the sensual satisfaction that both he and she herself can derive from their lovemaking.

The metaphors that follow are quite tantalizing. The woman's breasts are first characterized as date clusters found high up in the palm tree. They are then compared to clusters of grapes whose luscious taste is intoxicating. Here (v. 8) the man is enraptured by the taste of her breasts; later (v. 9) it will be her mouth (*ḥēk*, palate) that intoxicates him. This link between wine and erotic pleasure has been made frequently throughout the Song of Songs (1:2, 4; 4:10; 5:1). The sweet taste of her breasts and her mouth is then coupled with the sweet smell of her nose.[24] This particular sensory delight may not tantalize contemporary lovers, but it seems to have been quite common in the ancient world. It might be a reference to either nose-kissing or passionate breathing, both of which can be appropriately linked to the sweetness of the woman's palate (5:16; also 2:3; 4:11). This is an intoxication that can only be produced by the best of wine. The Hebrew construction is an expression of the superlative. Perhaps the allusion is to deep, passionate, open-mouth kissing.

---

[24] *ʾap*, which usually means "nose," could also mean "nipple." It is translated "vulva" by Pope, *Song of Songs*, 637–8. The NRSV renders it "breath" (7:8).

Desire Realized: 7:9b-13 [MT 7:10b-14]

Although 7:9 appears to be a single sentence, the appearance of the word *dôdî*,[25] which is the woman's favorite epithet for the man, suggests that she interrupts his speech at this point. He has been praising her, and she playfully picks up his words to affirm them:

He: "Your kisses are like the best wine . . ."

She: ". . . that flows smoothly for my beloved (*dôdî*),
down past the lips and teeth."

Although there is some disagreement about the exact translation of the words assigned to her, most versions agree that she admits that her kisses are indeed like wine that tantalizes the taste buds as it moves smoothly over them and creates a lulling effect in the one enjoying their intoxication. This is followed by part of the formula of mutual possession, though here it is inverted (2:16; 6:3). Also reversed is the desire (*těšûqâ*) for the loved one that is experienced. In the creation account it is the woman whose desire is for the man (Gen 3:16); here it is the man who desires her. In both cases, the desire is clearly a sexual one. However, here the word is not accompanied by the notion of dominion. This is mutual love, not an unequal relationship. It is interesting to note that whenever this formula appears, it is found in the mouth of the woman. She is clearly desirous of mutual possession.

The woman's invitation to a tryst begins and ends with the familiar term of endearment *dôdî*, (vv. 11, 13). A structure can be discerned in the first part of this invitation to tryst (vv. 11-12). It begins with the imperative "Come." This is followed by four first-person plural cohortatives ("let us"). The fourth cohortative leads into a series of three dependent clauses, each describing a sign of the burgeoning of spring:

Come, let us go forth

let us lodge

let us go out early

let us see whether vines have budded

blossoms have opened

pomegranates are in bloom.

The verb forms reflect the mutuality that marks the movement here.

[25] The NRSV's emendation of 7:9b [MT 7:10b] eliminates the word. The Hebrew reads "that flows smoothly for my beloved. . . ."

The woman invites the man to go out into the fields. The word *sādeh* denotes an open uncultivated area outside of a walled city. This was where the vineyards were normally planted, the place where so many trysts occurred. While the verb *lîn* simply means "to spend the night," the sexual implications are obvious. Finally, an explicit invitation into the vineyards brings to mind all of the earlier sensuous references and allusions to vineyards (1:14; 2:15), to vines (2:13; 6:11; 7:8), and to wine (1:2, 4; 4:10; 5:1; 7:9). Although some versions have "villages," *kĕpārîm* can also be translated "henna bushes" (1:14; 4:13). Actually, the second translation makes more sense in this context. If they have ventured into the fields, they would be less likely to retire to villages (plural) than to spend the night among the henna blossoms, which were frequently found in the uncultivated fields. From there they could easily go early into the vineyards.

The first three cohortative verbs invite movement toward a place; the fourth is an invitation to observe the signs of spring. The purpose of the visit to the vineyards is to observe the progress of spring growth. There are obvious links between this passage and the one describing the woman's visit to the nut orchard (6:11). In fact, two of the three signs of spring are identical to what the woman sought when she visited that garden: the budding of the vines and the pomegranates in bloom (v. 12; compare 6:11). Added here is the opening of the grape blossoms, a sign that is very similar to the other two. Her invitation also has much in common with the man's earlier request that the woman come out into the burgeoning new life of springtime (2:10-13). Despite the similarities between these two invitations, there are differences as well. In the earlier passage (2:10-13), spring had already awakened, and the man hoped that its surge of life would also awaken the love of the couple. In this verse (7:13), the love of the couple has already been well established, and they are in search of the signs of the awakening of springtime that might reflect their own love's surge of life. Together these passages show that spring is both actively involved in bringing forth human love and a mirror that symbolically reflects that love.

It is there in that place of flowering life that the woman will give the man her love. The word for love is plural in form and, as has been the case with its other appearances (1:2, 4; 4:10), is probably better translated "lovemaking." There is a play on words between "my love" (*dōday* [v. 12]) and mandrakes (*dûdā'îm* [v. 13]), the beautiful purple flowers that produce juicy, golden fruit. This exotic plant was considered an aphrodisiac and was associated with fertility (see Gen 30:14-16). The fragrance that it gives off is quite distinctive and, presumably, provocative. Once again, there is an allusion to the erotic nature of the sense of smell (1:2-3, 12-14; 4:10, 14, 16; 5:5). As the woman gives *(nātan)* her lovemaking, so the mandrakes give *(nātan)* their exotic fragrance.

The reference to the doorways (v. 14) is puzzling, since all of the references in this poem have been to the out-of-doors. Some commentators maintain that it is an allusion to the house of the woman's mother that will be mentioned in what follows (8:2). Others think that it is an entrance to the natural arbor suggested at the very beginning of the Song of Songs (1:17). What is clear is that these doorways are decorated with all of the choicest fruits. Since in an earlier poem the choicest fruits were really the physical charms of the woman (4:13, 16), the same meaning can be presumed here. The abundance of the fruits is seen in the phrase "new and old." It is a literary construction called merism, a form that implies totality by naming opposing poles (e.g., good and evil, north and south, left and right, etc.). The poles set the parameters of the object under consideration; the merism includes the poles and whatever is between them. The woman has already promised to make love (7:13). Here she declares that she has laid up the pleasures of lovemaking for her beloved *(dôdî)*.

A Secret Rendezvous: 8:1-4

This last segment of the fifth and longest unit of the Song of Songs is a song of fervent yearning. The scene has changed dramatically; gone are the references to the verdant springtime (7:10-13 [MT 7:11-14]) or the rich harvest (7:7-8 [MT 7:8-9]). The location about which the woman fantasizes is the house of her mother. There the lovers could satisfy their passionate desires uninhibited by the scrutinizing eyes of others. Despite this desire for privacy, the woman wishes for a situation where they could be able to express their love continuously and spontaneously, without having to flee for cover whenever they were overcome with desire. To this end, she wishes that they were brother and sister. Although he lovingly called her "sister" several times (4:9, 10, 12; 5:1, 2), this is the only time that she speaks of him as a brother, and then it is not as an epithet. What she desires is the freedom that the brother-sister relationship would afford them, a relationship which seems to have permitted public displays of affection without suspicion of prostitution or adultery (see Prov 7:10-13). The thought of the man suckling her mother's breasts as her brother would have done carries the idea of his suckling her own while in a passionate embrace (compare 7:8 [MT 7:9]).

Some commentators have wondered why, in this situation, the woman would be concerned with social mores when she spurned them in so many other situations described in the various poems. It should be remembered that, while she gave little thought to her own reputation, she was always careful to protect his. Public kissing would not only have led to her being despised, but it would have also cast a shadow on the man's propriety. All of this indicates that the couple were neither married nor betrothed to each other.[26]

This poem has much in common with two other passages that speak of a romantic rendezvous in a house (3:1-5; 5:2-8). All three passages mention precarious encounters with the public, and all three end with an adjuration to the daughters of Jerusalem. The verb *māṣāʾ* ("meet" or "find," v. 1), appears four times in 3:1-4 and three times in 5:6-8, the two accounts that report the woman's night ventures into the city in search of the man she loves. The first part of the verse that identifies the enclosure into which she would lead her love ("into the house of my mother") is the same as in 3:4. Some commentators even emend the second part of the verse in order to make it correspond with the first half.[27] Such emendation does not seem to be necessary, since it would be quite common for the woman to turn to her mother for advice in matters of the heart (see Ruth 3:1-5).[28]

The woman's amorous intentions are identified; she is interested in lovemaking. The text says that she will serve him wine. The relationship between wine and lovemaking has already been seen several times throughout the poems (1:2, 4; 4:10; 7:9 [MT 7:10]). Here the almost identical sound of the verbs serves to strengthen that relationship (*ʾašqĕkā*, "I will give you to drink"; *ʾeššāqĕkā*, "I will kiss you" [8:1]). It is not enough that she will offer him intoxicating wine, but it will be spiced wine, intended for erotic arousal. The juxtaposition of the spiced wine with the fruit of the pomegranate demonstrates this. Both were considered aphrodisiacs. However, they are probably to be understood metaphorically here, since the desire of both the man and the woman is so great that neither of them would need to indulge in any form of inebriation intended to incline them to lovemaking.

A twofold refrain (vv. 3-4) brings this poem of yearning and indeed the entire unit to a close. It repeats phrases found in both 2:6-7 and 3:5, and it does so in the same order as they appear in those earlier poems. However, in this instance mention of the gazelles and wild does is omitted, and *mah* ("what") is substituted for *ʾim* ("not"). This kind of

---

[26] This throws into question the notion that the poems that the Song of Songs comprises were originally wedding songs.

[27] See Pope, *Song of Songs,* 658–9; Fox, *Song of Songs,* 166.

[28] See Gordis, *Song of Songs,* 98; Landy, *Paradoxes of Paradise,* 100, 250; Bloch and Bloch, *Song of Songs,* 210.

repetition, referred to as associative sequence, is the recurrence of groups of words, sentences, or themes in the same order, even though such order does not seem to be required by the literary context or for the development of thought.[29] The first part of the refrain (v. 3; compare 2:6) describes an amorous embrace that should satisfy the longing of the lovers. The situation that the woman has sketched in her statement of desire is right for this embrace. In it, the man takes the woman into his arms and caresses her. This would be a fitting response to the demonstration of love that she wishes to bestow upon him.

There is a slight difference in the adjuration addressed to the daughters of Jerusalem that could make a significant difference in interpretation. Most commentators maintain that *mah* is used here as a negative, thus keeping the sense of the statement the same as it is in the earlier passages. However, a few do insist that it be understood as an interrogative.[30] Were this the case, it would mean that the daughters have already aroused love. Such a reading would credit them with a circumstance over which they clearly have no control. What would they be able to do that might arouse the love shared by the couple? Most likely, the woman is beseeching them not to interfere in the love that she shares with her loved one.

---

[29] Fox, *Song of Songs*, 215–7.
[30] Exum, "Literary and Structural Analysis," 74.

LOVE AFFIRMED
(8:5-14)

This final unit of the Song of Songs (8:5-14) is a composite of disparate questions and poems with catchwords and declarations that recall earlier scenes from the Song of Songs and that bring the entire collection to a conclusion. It is contained within an inclusion formed by *dôdâ* ("her beloved," v. 5a) and *dôdî* ("my beloved," v. 14). It opens with a statement of admiration in the form of an unanswered question (v. 5a) asked by an unidentified speaker. This is followed by a poem in praise of love spoken by the woman (vv. 5b-7). Next her brothers challenge her and she replies with a short poem that boasts of her maturity (vv. 8-10). There is a boasting statement by the man (vv. 11-12), and the unit and the Song of Songs itself ends with a dialogue between the man and the woman, expressing their desire for each other (vv. 13-14).

Out of the Wilderness: 8:5a

The question asked in the first part of the first colon of this verse is identical to one asked in an earlier poem (3:6a).[1] In both instances the questioner is unidentified. However, the earlier query was followed by the description of a magnificent procession coming out of the wilderness. Here it is followed by a simple clause that is much more suggestive than the earlier elaborate description. It is the lovers who emerge from the wilderness, and she is pressed up against him. The statement itself indicates an abrupt change of setting. In the poems immediately preceding it, the woman vividly described the vineyards bursting with life and then suggested the seclusion that the home of her mother

[1] A similar question is found in 6:10.

promises. This question implies that the lovers were in the wilderness (*midbār*) not the open field (*sādeh*). Although in other biblical passages the open field is considered a wilderness (compare Isa 43:20; Joel 1:20), here it is clearly a place of verdant growth. The second part of the colon contains a *hapax*. However, the root of the verb means "to support," and so the meaning intended here is clear. The scene is unmistakable, the lovers have been united and now they come up from the wilderness together.

There are two obvious features in this colon that link it to other parts of the Song of Songs. First, the question itself is a repetition of the earlier formula (3:6). Second, the image of the man supporting the woman is found both here and in the previous poem (8:3). This suggests that the poet is deliberately making connections, bringing the collection of poems to a conclusion.

The Power of Love: 8:5b-7

Neither the form nor the content of this poem flows easily from what precedes it. The masculine pronominal suffixes found in v. 5b indicate that it is the woman who is speaking. The perfect tenses of the verbs signify the recall of events from the past. Since the word for "awaken" (*ʿûr*) implies the arousal of passion rather than mere rousing from sleep when it is used in the adjurations to the daughters of Jerusalem (2:7; 3:5; 8:4), it should be understood with that same meaning here.[2] The sexual allusion is also present in the mention of the apple tree, a metaphor that the woman used in an earlier poem to characterize the man. She stated that she sat in his shadow and delighted in the sweetness of his fruit (2:3, 5). There she was aroused by him; here he is aroused by her.

There is a third sexual allusion in this verse. The woman claims that it was under this very tree that the man's mother conceived him. The verb *ḥābal* (compare 3:4) can mean either "to conceive" (see Ps 7:15) or "to bring forth in travail" (see Isa 13:8; 26:17). The very ambiguity of the word allows for both a literal and a metaphorical meaning. It is highly unlikely that the man's mother would have given birth in the open, under a tree, although it is quite possible that she could have conceived him there. However, divine births often took place under sacred trees,[3] and it is a fact that animals frequently mate in long-

---

[2] *Contra* Fox, *Song of Songs*, 168.
[3] Pope, *Song of Songs*, 663.

established breeding places. Since the man is characterized as a gazelle or a young stag, the woman could be speaking figuratively here as well. Whatever the case may be, just as her thoughts frequently return to her own mother's chamber (3:4; 8:2), there to enjoy erotic pleasures, so here the woman associates the couple's trysting site with the place where the man was conceived or brought forth.

Verse 6 is considered by many to be the most important statement of the entire Song of Songs. With an impassioned plea, the woman reveals the intensity of her desire. She asks to be a seal on her lover's heart, a seal on his arm. Seals were symbols of personal identity; they were frequently cylindrical in shape and worn around the neck so as to be near the heart (see Gen 38:18), or sometimes as a scarab stamp seal in the form of a ring (see Jer 22:24; Hag 2:23). Both kinds could be worn on the wrist or as an armband.[4] The woman's desire to be carried near the heart of her lover is understandable. However, since she speaks of a seal on his arm as well as one around his neck, the place of the seal seems less important than the meaning for which it stood.

The woman is not speaking of an amulet worn for protection or of some form of jewelry worn as adornment. Instead, she is referring to a kind of personal seal that had deep symbolic significance. It represented the owner's authority, honor, very identity. Nor is she asking that she might have such a seal. She wants to *be* the seal herself. She wants the union that they share to be so intimate that she might represent to others the very identity of her beloved. With such a request, she places herself in jeopardy in two ways. First, she risks the possibility that the man might not want to be publicly identified in this way. Second, she has no idea how the public will respond to this. It is obvious from the sentiments found throughout the poems that there is no risk in the first situation, and the woman cares little about the second. She is secure in their love and unconcerned about public opinion.

The statement about love contains three metaphors that describe some dimension of its depth and lasting endurance (vv. 6b-7). This is a statement about love in general, not specifically about the passion shared by this woman and this man. However, as is so often the case, deep and genuine love, though particular and unique in itself, gives one insight into the very nature of love in general. Many of the metaphors used to describe love have likened it to the surging powers of life. In a most unusual shift of perspective, the woman now compares it to the powers of death.[5]

[4] Keel, *Song of Songs*, 271–2.
[5] Author's translation.

(v. 6)	strong	as death	is love
	fierce	as the grave	is ardor
	Its sparks		are sparks of fire
			an enormous flame[6]

In this parallel construction, death and the grave refer to the same reality. But just what is the power to which love is compared? The tenor of the metaphors can hardly be the destructive power of death, for that would be a total contradiction to all of the metaphors describing love as life-giving or life-enhancing. The point of comparison is probably not the inevitability of death either, because there is no guarantee that one will be given the gift of love by another. The images of fire tell us that the focus here is on the consuming nature of love, which gives off flames or flashes of fire that flare with an elemental force (compare Prov 30:16). From this we may conclude that the tenor of the metaphor is the consuming nature of death.

This is not to say that death is a fiery experience, but rather that death and fire are unrelenting, and they take total possession of the person. Love resembles them in this way. As with death and fire, there are no half measures where there is real love. The poem does not say that love will eventually conquer death, or even that love and death are vying with each other in some kind of contest. Rather, it claims that just as death and the grave are tenacious and undaunted in the pursuit of their goals, so love is single-minded and undeterred in its pursuit of its goals.

Šeʾôl ("grave") is the name for the underworld. There are other mythological nuances behind some of the references in this comparison. The Hebrew words *môt* ("death") and *rešep* ("flame") are also the names of Canaanite deities. In Ugaritic literature, *Môt* is the mortal enemy of Baal, the god of fertility. Each year in the fall Baal was believed to have been devoured by *Môt*, only to be brought back to life in the spring through the passion of his sister-consort Anath. *Rešep* was a chthonic god of pestilence, represented in iconography holding arrows. With his fiery darts he afflicted humankind with plagues and various other scourges. Comparing the strength of love to these more-than-human realities suggests that there is nothing in this world that can compare with the power of love. In fact, it is not only otherworldly, but also able to withstand otherworldly assaults.

[6] The word ends with *yah*, a shortened form of the name of God. However, most commentaries argue that it is used here to express intensity or the superlative. (Translation of the verse is based on the NRSV, modified by the author.)

Reference to waters (v. 7) corroborates the meaning of this metaphor:

mighty waters	cannot quench	love
rivers	cannot drown	it

On the purely literal level, one can say that many waters cannot quench the blazing fire of love. However, there are mythological nuances here as well. Both *mayīm* ("waters") and *nāhār* ("river") are associated with Yamm, the Ugaritic god of chaotic cosmic waters. These waters were restrained by the creator god at the time of creation, but never completely subdued. They are always struggling to free themselves and to release chaos onto the world. Read with this background in mind, the woman is claiming that not even the mythological powers of chaos can dampen the flames of true love. Such love is steadfast and resistant to death, to the grave, to cosmic forces, to destruction of any kind, even to the forces of chaos.[7] Fragments of ancient creation myths tell of, and extant artifacts depict, cosmic battles among the gods. There we find weather gods using arrows of lightning to wage war against death, the sea and the river, and these weather gods emerge triumphant. The use of this imagery in the characterization of love is quite significant. It implies that human love, like the mythological weather gods, is able to withstand anything and everything.

These images all characterize human love as beyond the power and control of cosmic forces of chaos. The final phrase in this segment (v. 7cd) insists that it is futile to try to buy love, even if one is willing to risk all else to acquire it. This argument seems to be out of place, for, if love cannot be overwhelmed by powers beyond the human realm, it certainly cannot be bought with mere human resources. The wealth referred to is ordinary material goods or property *(hôn)*, not the bride-price *(mōhar)* that the man brings to marriage. This is not a reference to customary exchange. It is a statement about what an individual is willing to give *(nātan)* for the sake of love. The assertion concludes by insisting that anyone who even attempts such an undertaking would be despised, precisely for the reason given above. Not even all the goods of one's household can secure something that is beyond the control of cosmic forces. To think otherwise is to be foolish and deserving of scorn.

Scorn or contempt *(bûz)* links this passage with the one describing the fate of the woman should she kiss her lover in public (8:1). This is another example of how the last segment of this unit picks up vocabulary and imagery found in earlier poems and ties things together.

---

[7] This same language is used to describe the kind of security that God promises the faithful will enjoy in the eschatological age.

The Little Sister Matured: 8:8-10

There are many uncertainties in this short passage. This has led to various interpretations.[8] In every other instance where the woman is referred to as sister, it is the man who is using that designation as a term of endearment (4:9, 10, 12; 5:1, 2). Various features indicate that the man is not the speaker here. Most obvious among these is the first person possessive plural form of the pronoun. Second, the woman is referred to as "little" *(qĕṭannâ)*, a word that denotes not only small in size but insignificant in value. Her lover would never speak of her in this way. Finally, the description of the woman's breasts contradicts the praise that the man accorded them in earlier poems (4:5; 7:3, 7, 8 [MT 7:4, 8, 9]). Most likely the speakers are the brothers who were mentioned at the beginning of the Song of Songs (1:6).

The brothers' concern for their sister reflects the question of her eligibility for marriage. A brother's involvement in arranging the marriage of his sister is a well-established custom in many patriarchal societies. We see this in various instances within the biblical tradition itself (Laban and Rebecca in Gen 24:29-60; the sons of Jacob and Dinah in Gen 34:6-17; the men and women of Shiloh in Judg 21:22). The brothers seemed concerned about carrying out this responsibility when their sister is of the age to be "spoken for" or wooed. Developed breasts and the appearance of pubic hair were signs of puberty and signaled the woman's physical preparedness for marriage (see Ezek 16:7). The brothers' claim that she has no breasts indicates that they consider her sexually immature and not ready for marriage, an assessment that is diametrically opposed to the way the man has perceived his loved one throughout the poems.

Having questioned their sister's readiness for marriage, the brothers next suggest ways to protect her marriageability. This second concern reflects the importance of safeguarding a woman's reproductive potential, from which would be born the heir of the property and movable goods. It was important that the inheritance be handed down through the correct line of descent. For this reason, a woman who engaged in inappropriate sexual relations was either physically punished or considered by some as unmarriageable. The restriction of women was less for the sake of their virginity than for the safety of the family inheritance. In this passage the brothers consider ways of safeguarding their sister's marriageability. The man has already compared her to two glorious capital cities of ancient Israel, Tirzah and Jerusalem. Here her brothers pick up aspects of a city and employ them in their description

[8] See Pope, *Song of Songs,* 678–86; Fox, *Song of Songs,* 171–2.

of her. The two conditional phrases that characterize their musings (v. 9) are in strict parallel construction, each word of the first clause having a counterpart in the second:

a   If she (is) a wall

b   we will build on her

c   a battlement of silver

a'   If she (is) a door

b'   we will enclose her

c'   with boards of cedar

Some commentators believe that the parallelism is synonymous, containing analogous military metaphors describing a city's defenses.[9] They consider wall and door as restrictions that prohibit entrance. Other interpreters read it as antithetic parallelism with metaphors of opposite meaning.[10] They agree that the wall prevents access, but they believe that the door allows it. Since the Hebrew word is door *(delet)* and not doorway *(petaḥ;* see 7:13b [MT 7:14b]), the first interpretation is preferred here. Whichever understanding is adopted, the character and intent of the metaphors are fundamentally the same. The harshness of military imagery is qualified by the addition of precious adornments that signal the extraordinary value and beauty of the woman. The man used a similar poetic device when he likened the woman's neck to the tower of David embellished with military banners (4:4).

Comparing their sister to a wall, the brothers would not only fortify her with a parapet, thus securing her integrity, but they would use silver in its construction, thus establishing her beauty. Comparing her to a door, they would reinforce the door with boards of cedar, wood that is both strong and precious. Both metaphors reflect the woman's inaccessibility and her brothers' willingness to reinforce that inaccessibility, while at the same time making her even more desirable. As was stated in the earlier passage that mentioned them (1:6), they feel their social responsibility for the oversight of her sexual conduct, and they intend to take measures that they think are appropriate to safeguard her marriageability.

While the text is not clear as to the audience of the brothers' pronouncement, it is their sister who responds to them. As has been the case throughout the Song of Songs, she needs no one to direct her future,

[9] See Fox, *Song of Songs,* 172; Elliott, *Literary Unity,* 202; Keel, *Song of Songs,* 278.
[10] See Murphy, *Song of Songs,* 198; Bloch and Bloch, *Song of Songs,* 215–7.

to assess her potential, to attend to her needs. At least where the love she shares with the man is concerned, she is in control of the circumstances of her life. Using the very imagery that they used, she challenges her brothers' assessment of her physical maturity. She claims that she is indeed nubile. She further states that she is a wall; she has been inaccessible (4:12). Because she has enjoyed some of the pleasures of lovemaking does not mean that she has been open to anyone other than her lover. In earlier poems various parts of her body had been compared to towers: her neck was adorned like the embellished tower of David (4:4); it was also characterized as a stately and elegant tower of ivory (7:4 [MT 7:5]); her nose was said to be straight like a tower of Lebanon (7:4 [MT 7:5]). In this connection with earlier imagery, she claims that her breasts are so developed that they resemble towers, an image that is no more exaggerated than any other metaphor used to describe her body.

Any interpretation of the obscure ending of this verse can only be tentative. Since the woman has been contesting her brothers' estimation of her, she can hardly be claiming that she has finally found favor in their eyes.[11] Also contested is the meaning of the verb *yāṣāʾ* ("go out"). Some argue for "finds peace,"[12] while others read it as "brings peace."[13] The second rendering is preferred here. Her rebuttal would insist that it is precisely because of her maturity and the integrity that has been strengthened through it, that the man she loves looks upon her as the one who brings peace. This is the only time that the word peace *(šālôm)* appears in the Song of Songs. It is a link with the references to Solomon that follow.

Solomon's Vineyard: 8:11-12

This short poem is a boasting song sung by the man. It begins with a description of a vineyard owned by Solomon and then compares the royal vineyard with one that belongs to the man. Although the change in speaker and content clearly sets this section off from what immediately precedes it, the poem does not stand isolated from the rest of the Song of Songs. There are at least two links with the previous passage. The first is linguistic. The last word in the preceding verse *(šālôm,*

---

[11] So argues Fox, *Song of Songs*, 173.

[12] See Fox, *Song of Songs*, 173; Murphy, *Song of Songs*, 193; Bloch and Bloch, *Song of Songs*, 217–8.

[13] Pope, *Song of Songs*, 683–6.

"peace") comes from the same root as does the name of the great Judean king Solomon *(Šĕlōmōh)*. The second link is thematic. Both passages acclaim the incomparable value of the woman.

Like other verses in this last unit, this passage also picks up several themes found in earlier poems. Besides the appearance of the name in the superscription of the book (1:1), there are two other references to Solomon himself (3:9, 11) and two to decorations associated with him (1:5; 3:7). Vineyard appears several times (1:6; 2:15; 6:11; 7:12 [MT 7:13]) and vineyard keepers play a role in the beginning of the Song of Songs (1:6) as well as here at the end.

The opening statement, "Solomon had a vineyard," is reminiscent of the narrative poem that identifies Israel as the vineyard of God (see Isa 5:1). The place name, Baal-hamon or Lord of the Multitude, probably has little to do with location, but is rather an allusion to Solomon's extensive holdings. Both the size of the vineyard and the personal dignity of the king precluded his own involvement in caring for the vineyard as keeper. Instead, like God in the Isaian poem, he entrusted his valuable vineyard to the keeping of others. The scope of the yield of this vineyard can be seen in the amounts of money exchanged. Each attendant was required to bring the owner a thousand pieces of silver for the fruit that was grown, a requirement that was probably not beyond the realm of possibility (see Isa 7:23). From this amount the attendants were allowed to keep some money for themselves. The scene sketched here resembles tenant farming and sharecropping, a very common practice in the ancient Near Eastern world.

In contrast to the king who shares with others not only his vineyard but also the fruits that it produces, the man boasts that his own vineyard is for him alone. It may not compare in size or yield with that of the king, but it is his and his alone. He shares the fruits of this vineyard with no one. Although this reference can be understood to mean an actual vineyard, it also has metaphorical significance. In the very beginning of the Song of Songs, the woman characterized herself as a vineyard (1:6). It seems that now the man is doing the same thing, thus adding vineyard to the descriptions of her as a garden locked and a fountain sealed (4:12) as well as a fortified wall and a closed door. The one aspect that all of these images have in common is the woman's inaccessibility to everyone but the man she loves.

If the man's vineyard is really a symbol for the woman, then surely the king's vineyard stands for something else as well. The deliberate contrast between the two vineyards suggests that if one is a symbol so is the other. It has been suggested by some that it is an allusion to the royal harem. This would explain the name of the place (Lord of the Multitude). On the other hand, this extravagance might be simply a way of insisting that not even extensive royal wealth is capable of procuring genuine love, a view that reinforces a similar statement made earlier (8:7).

The Final Exchange: 8:13-14

This final passage has much in common with 2:14-17. All of the forms of the words in verse 13 tell us that it is the woman who is being addressed. The vocabulary in the last verse indicates that it is to the man that she responds. The imagery of vineyard gives way to that of garden. Although elsewhere garden often represents the woman, here it should be understood literally. Throughout the poems garden has signified an enclosure that produces a vast array of fruits that delight sight, taste, smell, and touch. To say that the woman dwells in such gardens is to suggest that she not only enjoys the fecundity and beauty of nature, but that she participates in it. There may even be the implication that she herself rewards with comparable delights the one who partakes of her charms.

The man states that his companions too are listening for her voice. These companions could be the same ones mentioned in the beginning of the Song of Songs, those who were with the man out in the fields with their flocks (1:7). Why they should be listening for her voice is unclear. The primary focus of the phrase is not their listening, but the listening of the man. It is he who longs to hear her voice. His request is the same as one posed earlier: "Let me hear your voice" (2:14). The Hebrew implies that it is the sound of her voice *(qôl)* and not any particular message that she might speak that is the object of his desire. The man's longing is obvious.

The woman's response has been interpreted in various ways. It is very similar to the way she responded to the man's earlier request to hear her voice: "Turn, my beloved, be like a gazelle or a young stag on the cleft mountains" (2:17). However, there are significant differences between the two responses. The verb used in the earlier passage is *sōb,* which can mean either "turn away from" or "return to." Here the verb *bārah* clearly means "to bolt" or "to run away from." Is she asking him to flee from her? Or from the companions of whom he spoke? In the earlier passage, the mountain *(beṭer)* was difficult to identify. We have already seen that some commentators maintain that this is the proper name of a specific but unknown mountain, or a spice-producing location. Others believe that it is an allusion to the breasts of the woman. Since there is an allusion to her breasts in yet another reference to mountain ("mountain of myrrh, hill of frankincense," 4:6), and since her charms are frequently compared to spices, one can safely conclude that the "mountain of spices" mentioned here is an allusion to the woman as well. All of this suggests that she is entreating the man *(dôdî)* to escape from his companions and with great haste to come to her.

In this way the Song of Songs ends, not with final consummation of the passionate love that is described throughout its many individual poems, but on a note of separation with a plea for union. As incomplete as this may sound, it is also quite true of authentic love. Human love knows no definitive consummation, no absolute fulfillment. Loving relationships are never complete; they are always ongoing, always reaching for more. Regardless of the quality or frequency of lovemaking, there is always a measure of yearning present.

WORKS CITED

Alonso Schökel, Luis. *A Manual of Hebrew Poetics*. Subsidia Biblica 11. Rome: Editrice Pontificio Istituto Biblico, 1988.

Berlin, Adele. *The Dynamics of Biblical Parallelism*. Bloomington, IN: Indiana University Press, 1985.

Bloch, Ariel, and Chad Bloch. *The Song of Songs*. New York: Random House, 1995.

Botterweck, Johannes G., and Helmer Ringgren, eds. *Theological Dictionary of the Old Testament*. Vol. III. Grand Rapids: Eerdmans, 1978.

Brenner, Athalya. *The Song of Songs*. Sheffield: JSOT Press, 1989.

Carr, Lloyd G. *The Song of Solomon: An Introduction and Commentary*. Tyndale Old Testament Commentaries. Downers Grove, IL: InterVarsity Press, 1984.

Copher, Charles B. "The Black Presence in the Old Testament." *Stony the Road We Trod*. Ed. Cain Hope Felder, 146–64. Philadelphia: Fortress, 1991.

Deckers, M. "The Structure of the Song of Songs and the Centrality of *nepeš* (6: 12)." *A Feminist Companion to the Song of Songs*. Ed. Athalya Brenner, 172–96. Sheffield: JSOT Press, 1993.

Elliott, M. Timothea. *The Literary Unity of the Canticle*. European University Series 23. Bern: Peter Lang, 1989.

Exum, J. Cheryl. "A Literary and Structural Analysis of the Song of Songs." *Zeitschrift für die alttestamentliche Wissenschaft* 8 (1973) 47–79.

Falk, Marcia. *The Song of Songs: A New Translation and Interpretation*. Old Testament Guides. San Francisco: HarperCollins, 1990.

Fox, Michael V. *The Song of Songs and the Ancient Egyptian Love Songs*. Madison: University of Wisconsin Press, 1985.

Freedman, D. N. "Acrostics and Metrics in Hebrew Poetry." *Harvard Theological Review* 65 (1972) 367–92.

Gordis, Robert. *The Song of Songs*. New York: Jewish Theological Seminary of America Press, 1981.

Goulder, Michael D. *The Song of Fourteen Songs*. Sheffield: JSOT Press, 1986.

Keel, Othmar. *The Song of Songs*. A Continental Commentary. Fortress Press, 1994.

Kugel, James L. *The Idea of Biblical Poetry: Parallelism and Its History*. New Haven: Yale University Press, 1981.

Landy, Francis. *Paradoxes of Paradise: Identity and Difference in the Song of Songs*. Bible and Literature Series 7. Sheffield: Almond Press, 1983.

Lowth, Robert. *De sacra poesi Hebraeorum*. London: Oxford Press, 1753.

Mariaselvam, Abraham. *The Song of Songs and Ancient Tamil Love Poems: Poetry and Symbolism*. Analecta Biblica 118. Rome: Editrice Pontificio Istituto Biblico, 1988.

Matter, Ann E. *The Voice of My Beloved: The Song of Songs in Western Medieval Christianity*. Philadelphia: University of Pennsylvania Press, 1990.

Munro, Jill M. *Spikenard and Saffron: A Study in the Poetic Language of the Song of Songs*. Journal for the Study of the Old Testament Supplement Series 203. Sheffield: Sheffield Academic Press, 1995.

Murphy, Roland E. *The Song of Songs*. Hermeneia. Minneapolis: Fortress Press, 1990.

————. *Wisdom Literature: Job, Proverbs, Ruth, Canticles, Ecclesiastes, and Esther*. The Forms of the Old Testament Literature 13. Grand Rapids: Eerdmans, 1981.

O'Connor, M. *Hebrew Verse Structure*. Winona Lake, IN: Eisenbrauns, 1980.

Pardes, Ilana. *Countertraditions in the Bible*. Cambridge, MA: Harvard University Press, 1992.

Pope, Marvin. *The Song of Songs*. Anchor Bible 7C. Garden City, NY: Doubleday, 1977.

Rowley, Harold H. "The Interpretation of the Song of Songs." *The Servant of the Lord and Other Essays*. 2nd revised edition, 195–246. Oxford: Blackwell, 1965.

Shea, William H. "The Chiastic Structure of the Song of Songs." *Zeitschrift für die alttestamentliche Wissenschaft* 92 (1984) 378–96.

Snaith, John G. *The Song of Songs*. New Century Bible Commentary. Grand Rapids: Eerdmans, 1993.

Soulen, Richard N. "The *waṣf* of the Song of Songs and Hermeneutic." *Journal of Biblical Literature* 86 (1967) 183–90.

Stadelmann, Luis. *Love and Politics: A New Commentary on the Song of Songs*. New York: Paulist Press, 1992.

Tournay, Raymond Jacques. *Word of God, Song of Love*. Translated by J. Edward Crowley. New York: Paulist Press, 1988.

Watson, Wilfred G.E. *Classical Hebrew Poetry: A Guide to Its Techniques.* Sheffield: Sheffield Academic Press, 1995.

_____. *Traditional Techniques in Classical Hebrew Verse.* Sheffield: Sheffield Academic Press, 1994.

GENERAL INDEX

Abishag, 81
adjuration, xv, xvi, 26, 36, 59–60,
    66–8, 75, 93–4, 96
Africa, 55, 65
Akiba, vii, viii, 4
Akkadian, xii, xv, 11, 20, 65
allegory, x, xi
    ecclesiological, x
    mariological, x
    tropological, x
alliteration, xiii, 3, 14, 17, 31, 41, 51,
    53
Alonso Schökel, Luis, xii (n. 19)
Ambrose, ix
Amorite, 85
Anath, 98
aphrodisiac, 25, 55, 93
Aphrodite, 76
apple, 24–5, 96
Arabia, 14, 20, 55, 69
arms, 71
Asia, 55
associative sequence, 94
assonance, xiii, 31, 41
Assyrian, 66
asyndetic hendiadys, 69
authorship, vii, 3–4

Baal-hamon, 103
Bath-rabbim, 86
beauty, viii, xiv, 13–14, 18–19, 21–3,
    26, 33, 37–58, 59, 62, 68–73, 75–7,
    88, 101

belly, 71–2, 82–5
Berlin, Adele, xiii (n. 21; n. 22)
Bernard of Clairvaux, x
black, 13–14, 16, 19, 70
Bloch, Ariel, and Chad Bloch, 15
    (n. 10), 31 (n. 3), 38 (n. 1), 44 (n. 9),
    47 (n. 14), 67 (n. 17), 70 (n. 21),
    79 (n. 8), 93 (n. 28), 101 (n. 10),
    102 (n. 12)
Botterweck, Johannes G., and Helmer
    Ringgren, 11 (n. 5), 20 (n. 14)
breast, 18, 20–1, 24, 33, 43, 48–9, 82,
    84–5, 89, 92, 100, 104
Brenner, Athalya, x (n. 10)
bride, 11, 38–9, 49–52, 54, 56–7, 61
bridegroom, 11, 11 (n. 4), 38–9
brother, 15, 16, 52, 92, 95, 100–2

Canaanite, 98
canonicity, vii
Carmel, 87–8
Carr, Lloyd, G., xi (n. 11), 60 (n. 1),
    61 (n. 5), 68 (n. 18)
cola, xii
Copher, Charles B., 13 (n. 7)
cheek, 43, 71, 77
chiasm, xiv, 8, 27–8, 30–1, 41
city, 12, 16, 23, 26, 34–6, 60–1, 66, 74,
    76–7, 85–6, 91, 93
creation (nature), x, 5, 18
crown, viii, 41, 87
cult, viii, ix, x
Cyril of Alexandria, ix

INDEX OF HEBREW WORDS

INDEX OF SCRIPTURAL REFERENCES